# STARTING
# FROM
# SCRATCH

# STARTING FROM SCRATCH

## A Different Kind Of Writers' Manual

# RITA MAE BROWN

BANTAM BOOKS
NEW YORK · TORONTO · LONDON · SYDNEY · AUCKLAND

STARTING FROM SCRATCH
*A Bantam Book*
*Bantam hardcover edition / February 1988*
*Bantam trade edition / April 1989*

Library of Congress Cataloging-in-Publication Data

Brown, Rita Mae.
  Starting from scratch.

  Bibliography: p.
  1. Brown, Rita Mae—Authorship.   2. Authorship.
I. Title.
PS3552.R698Z47   1988      813´.54      87-19535
ISBN 0-553-34630-X

*Published simultaneously in the United States and Canada*

---

Bantam Books are published by Bantam Books, a division of Bantam
Doubleday Dell Publishing Group, Inc. Its trademark, consisting of the
words "Bantam Books" and the portrayal of a rooster, is Registered in
U.S. Patent and Trademark Office and in other countries. Marca Regis-
trada. Bantam Books, 1540 Broadway, New York, New York 10036.

---

"Scribble, scribble scribble! Eh, Mr. Gibbon?"
To you Scribblers everywhere

# CONTENTS

# INTRODUCTION

It's an act of faith to be a writer in a postliterate world. One disrobes one's typewriter with trembling and hope. Did someone put the film of history into the projector backwards? Are we becoming more barbaric and illiterate? Are we entering the technological Dark Ages?

If we are, then, as in the original Dark Ages, there will be people dedicated to Literature. We may be diminished in number but we won't die out, because a book will remain what it has ever been: the most intense, private form of communication between two minds. This special bond invests the act of reading and the act of writing with passion. Inevitably it becomes a love affair or its opposite.

This fiction writer's manual is not a substitute for the more conventional manuals. Rather, it gathers what I've learned the hard way through my failures and my occasional triumphs. I hope some of the following will be useful to you. If it isn't, don't tell me.

Every writer starts from the foundation of his or her physical life. We each carry beliefs formed in childhood that are so much a part of us as to be definitive. If I tell you mine, as a person and a writer, maybe you'll be able to decide whether to push on with this volume.

I believe all literature started as gossip. I believe self-pity stinks. I believe that a hen never cackles until she's finished her job. I believe in art that conceals art. I believe we often disguise pain through ritual and it may be the only solace we have. Literature is part of that ritual. I believe in a lively disrespect for most forms of authority. I believe every change any word has undergone probably originated in ignorance. I believe life is a grand spectacle of foolishness and that each generation must find its weapons for the old battle of good versus evil, life versus death, the trivial versus the profound. I believe that I have the ability to write a pulp novel larger than the Cedars of Lebanon and I hope I can resist the siren call to do it. I believe in serenity, not passivity. I believe that after exhausting all other alternatives, I'll behave reasonably.

While the above beliefs may not spill over into the information in this writer's manual, my temperament will. Best you know that before you embark, because if you can tolerate my temperament you'll probably enjoy the writer's manual. Even if you reject this book it will have served its purpose, which is to clarify your thinking and your feelings about writing. You'll at least know what you don't like, and that's a gift of sorts.

Being happy made me want to write, so I figured writing would make me happy. I set off to be a writer and my above-stated childhood premise proved correct. I have been writing since I was fifteen. I am now forty-one. I didn't make any money from my labor until I was twenty-eight and then I made $1,000. Still, writing made me happy. Now, years later, with a sprinkling of novels that clambered onto *The New York Times* Best Seller list, with two Emmy nominations under my belt and with contracts for future novels, teleplays, and screenplays in hand, I can say that writing not only makes me happy but brings me rapture. Happiness is in the animal brain and joy is in the cerebrum. Writing gives me both experiences of pleasure.

Notice I am not saying that the work is easy. I doubt any writer will tell you that but why dedicate yourself to something that's easy? I can't promise that writing will make you happy, but if you're the real thing you'll never be bored. That may be the greatest gift each of the Arts gives its practitioners. I hope that you may write on.

In order to help you do that, let me, up front, tell you something you need to know. Creativity comes from trust. Trust your instincts. And never hope more than you work.

Your far from humble servant,

RITA MAE BROWN

CHARLOTTESVILLE, VIRGINIA

# STARTING FROM SCRATCH

# I
## ME

# THE CHICKEN
## OR
## THE EGG?

Writers will happen in the best of families. No one is quite sure why. What comes first: the chicken or the egg—the family or the writer? Fortunately, this question cannot be answered, insuring grist for the biographer's mill whenever a deceased writer is the subject. Oscar Wilde said, "Biography lends to death a new terror." This is especially true for a writer because it's so easy to read far more than was intended into novels, plays, poetry.

Maybe you know why you are a writer. I don't know why I am. I only know it never occurred to me to be anything else, and I proudly display the stigmata of my novels as proof of this. Let me tell you how I started, not so much because I need to tell you but because my publisher wants to know. She needs an explanation for the torrent of words that flows across her desk. Also, she thinks you might want to know how one person started in this profession and managed to survive.

I wasn't kidding when I said I've never thought of being anything but a writer. I was born knowing. I think of birth as the search for a larger apartment. I wanted a huge apartment that was one big library. I started to read at three. Don't be alarmed if you did not begin so early. The reason I started was that I was blessed with a mother and father who encouraged me, read to me, told me stories, and did everything humanly possible to activate my mind.

It's silly to wait until first grade to teach children to read. They are ready before that.

I received my first library card at the age of five. My mother lied to the librarian and told her I was six because there was an age qualification for being issued a card. The first books I checked out of the Martin Library were Bulfinch's *Mythology*, Alcott's *Little Women*, and Strickland's *Queens of England, Volume I*. The librarian would not give me the books because she thought them too difficult for me. This so enraged my mother, Julia Ellen Brown (nee Buckingham), that she made me stand on a chair so that I could see the librarian and whisper to her from *Little Women*. I carried it off without a hitch and the lady let me have the books. After that, I spent almost every Saturday morning at this beautiful little library in York, Pennsylvania. Saturdays I was usually in the care of my father, Ralph Clifford Brown, and he would drop me at the library at nine in the morning, the minute the doors opened, and pick me up at lunchtime. After lunch I'd go to the store and work with Dad. I loved working with my father, a man with a forty-two-inch chest, a hand that could palm a basketball, and a baritone so deep and rich he made my backbone rattle when he sang.

At lunchtime, usually down at the market on Market Street, he would examine my books and we'd talk about them. We'd wrap the books in butcher paper so they wouldn't get dirty, because Dad and his two brothers had a stall in the market, Browns Meats. (The sign painter forgot the apostrophe.) Butchers get bloody and so do butchers' kids, so we were careful to protect each week's haul of books until I could get back home and properly wash up.

Some Saturdays I'd be with Mother, but the library ritual changed only in that Mother wouldn't let me linger. I had to snap up the books and go, because she wanted to walk all over York Square, nose around the shops and visit her friends. Mother enjoyed a lovely figure even to the day she died, at age seventy-eight and a half, because she would walk three to eight miles a day. It kept her young and full of curiosity. God forbid "Juts" should miss anything. So there I would be, hustling to keep up with Mom, and learning at an early age to watch people. I'd also get tired of carrying the books (I always checked out too many) and inevitably these would be dumped on Mother.

By the time I was in kindergarten Mother and Dad's friends told me I would be a writer. My kindergarten teacher told me that, too. What they saw, I don't know. But the idea of my being a writer was reinforced early.

School proved a problem. Violet Hill Elementary was small and served poor and working-class children. It still stands, but the fields around it, and the barn next door with the draft horses, have given way to houses. Development is the curse of our time. Anyway, I would finish my lessons quickly and then make trouble. This devilishness could have gotten me off to a bad start, but I was fortunate because my first-grade teacher, Miss Potter, figured out I was ahead of my classmates. Whenever I'd finish a lesson, I could turn it in and then go to the school library. I was allowed to do this until fourth grade, when I was transferred to Valley View Elementary School. I still don't know why I was transferred. Mother may have been behind this because Valley View was a bigger and better school, full of rich kids. On reflection I realize they were merely middle class but we did not possess much in the way of material things so these doctors' daughters and lawyers' sons seemed rich to me. I hated them too. They were competitive, snotty, and devious. They learned to hide their emotions early, to bow to authority without question, and to keep their allowances to themselves. I came from an opposing world view. I was taught to express myself (throw dishes if it came to that), to question authority, and to share what I had with my friends. I was also taught to stick to my own kind; by that, Mom and Dad meant to back up my friends. If your friend gets in a fight, even if he or she is wrong, you back your friend. You can argue with her later. How different for my little middle-class schoolmates, who would ditch their buddy in a minute if it was to their advantage or if the teacher bore down on them.

These memories are painted in primary colors because they

are childhood memories. I am not attempting to be fair to my
middle-class schoolmates. I am only telling you how they looked to
me at the time. Obviously, I now have much more sympathy for
children from the middle classes.

So I learned to hide my emotions and that meant to hide my
work. I didn't write stories at Valley View. I wrote them at home. I
did manage, with the help of Mother and Dad, to go to the library
when I was finished with my lessons but this took a semester to
accomplish. So for my first semester I sat in a state of advanced
boredom.

As the three years left to me in elementary school ground
down, I learned something extraordinary. I learned that other
mothers and fathers did not love one another. They were unhappy
and sometimes they ignored their own children. Strange as it may
sound now, this came as a deep shock to me. I knew only love.
Mom and Dad were crazy for each other and they didn't cover
it up. They loved me, too, but I was not the center of attention. They didn't try to be my best friend. They were my parents
and to them that meant teaching me right from wrong, teaching
me good work habits, and doing anything they could to get me
the best public education available. My every whim was most
definitely not granted. As the years pass I realize how lucky I
was to have such parents. They prepared me for the world. The rest
was up to me.

But the nagging specter of unhappy people affected me. I
wanted to know why they were unhappy. My reading took a turn. I
poured myself into Tolstoy (he specialized in unhappiness, it
seemed to me at that time), I devoured Dickens, and I ripped
through Dumas and then Hugo. I learned from these writers that
readers like surprises but not confusion. Tolstoy could get confusing. The sheer grandeur of his themes overcame this and his
stylistic shortcomings. (Perhaps he reads better in his native language. Most people do.) In contrast, Dumas's plots drove with
energy to their conclusion, but his themes were not as broad. I was
learning, but many times I would have to read novels three and

four times to grasp all I could of what they contained. I also continued my readings in mythology and the King James version of the Bible. I confess I had to read the Bible because of Sunday School and church but I did get a lot out of it. I still read mythology and the Bible.

I gleaned few answers as to why people were unhappy or why they couldn't love one another but I absorbed a lot about how to tell a crackling good story. At this time Mom and Dad did something that freed me. They moved, literally, out of the blue and at age fifty, to Fort Lauderdale, Florida. It was 1955 and you can't imagine how beautiful Florida was then, before they paved it over with concrete. The smells alone would intoxicate the most rigid of people: night-blooming jasmine, the tang of salt air, and the odd sandy smell after a driving rain. Overhead, creamy, imposing clouds sailed across brilliant blue skies, and the ocean—what colors: cobalt-blue, emerald-green, turquoise-blue, and light-hazel bands of color right next to one another. This was Nirvana. I was up at 6:30 A.M. and to bed at 10:00 P.M. Except for school I was outdoors most of the time. If I wasn't outside then I was downtown, at the old library on Middle River. A few years later, to my joy, the city of Fort Lauderdale constructed a big new library in Holiday Park. It was a mile and a half from my front door and I could walk to it. Once again I made friends with the librarians (what unsung heroines and heroes are librarians) and they allowed me in the stacks. I could go anywhere I wanted in the library. By now I was reading four to five books a week. I would buttonhole any librarian I could, to see if she (they were mostly women in those days) had read what I had just read. Do you know, in all the years I have haunted libraries I have never once been put down or turned away by a librarian when I have asked that question? Book lovers are really a tribe.

Also, back then Fort Lauderdale was a small town. The population wasn't but 45,000 people, depending on who was counting. People knew me, and my love of books and tennis preceded me. I had so many friends of all ages. My tennis partners were often in their sixties and seventies. They would bring books from their private libraries to me at Holiday Courts. (Before Holiday Courts there were a few pockmarked clay courts at South Side, so now I had the best tennis courts and the library practically at my doorstep.)

I started seventh grade at Naval Air. We used to joke that the only reason the wooden buildings were standing was because the termites held hands. Despite the termites I liked the school because I changed classrooms every hour. I also loved the environment. The teachers were tough on us, and in retrospect I think it was because Southern schools had such a bad rap. They overcompensated. Anyway, it was to my benefit—I'm not complaining.

There even was a little girl who used to follow me around the tennis courts—Christine Evert. She, her brother, Drew, and her sister, Jeannie, bring back floods of memories. Even those little kids carried their books to the courts.

I started writing in school again. I wrote the school play every year, or what passed for a school play. I wrote for the newspaper. I wrote for the yearbook. I couldn't stop and my classmates rewarded me for it by asking my opinion. Did I like this and what did I think of that and would I look at their term papers?

As an adult I know my freedom had to do with more than Florida's fabulous climate. It didn't occur to me until I was in my twenties that our move had freed me from the bonds of my illegitimacy. I was adopted. My natural father, a Venable (a Virginia family with a deep taproot in Charlottesville), was not married to my natural mother, a Young. Julia and Ralph Brown were fair people with beautiful gray eyes. Dad Brown had blond hair when young. There I was, with my dark hair, a living testimony to the persistence of Gallic genes. No one had to tell me. My natural father lived right there in York and my natural mother wasn't all that far away. In a fight at school the first word out of some kid's mouth was "bastard." Sure, I was good with my fists and eventually people let it lie, but I never forgot. In Fort Lauderdale no one cared. I had an equal chance. I made the most of it.

Oddly enough I have written about Fort Lauderdale only once, in my first novel, *Rubyfruit Jungle*. (I also used South Florida in *Sweet Surrender*, a feature film, musical, that I wrote for 20th Century-Fox.) I will return to Florida as a literary environment someday but until that time I can only say how much I loved it. The subtropics, really, are my natural habitat.

Dad gave me a huge Underwood typewriter when I was eight. He traded some meat for it. So by the time I was in high school my fingers could fly over the keys. If any of you reading this have ever worked on those old typewriters, you know how they were. You got forearms despite yourself and the little muscles in your hands became well developed also. My dad—I haven't even got enough adjectives for him, I loved him so much—also gave me a brand new Smith-Corona typewriter for my fifteenth birthday. It was powder-blue. Where did that man get the money? We didn't have two nickels to rub together and I'm not exaggerating. When Dad died on August 13, 1961, I was already filling out scholarship forms for college (to enter in 1962) and the combined incomes of Dad, Mom, and me came to $2,000. After Dad died we lost half our earning power. I still don't know what my father sacrificed to give me this wonderful typewriter.

I wrote poetry, newspaper stuff, and every now and then I would experiment with plays. I joined the city's Junior Theater, which was next to the railroad tracks on Flagler Drive. You could see the building from our pink house. Mostly I painted scenery because my acting talents were nil. And I listened to the readings. Our Junior Theater was big on musicals. Whatever was on Broadway we did. We also resurrected hits from the near past like *Brigadoon*, but our best show in those years was *Flower Drum Song*. I watched the school plays at Fort Lauderdale High, but since I was number one on the tennis team and my schedule conflicted with the theater group's, I couldn't participate. But I wrote plays for my class and sometimes for the whole school. My biggest hit was "Santa's Workshop," which I did for the city's crippled and sick children. We packed two thousand of them into War Memorial

Auditorium in Holiday Park, December 1961. Every time one of my favorite lines got a laugh I was thrilled. Hooked. By now I could no more stop writing than stop breathing.

By now I was also reading fluently in Latin and learning about new styles of writing. Because Latin is inflected (this is explained in the chapter on Latin) a writer can physically move words around without destroying grammar; the grammer is contained within the word ending. This gives rise to very different styles of writing than are possible in English. I loved Latin and I especially loved Horace. Then I started to read Latin plays, mostly Plautus and Terence. What an education. Now I had a vivid contrast to English and I wanted to sharpen my command of the language. The technical aspects of writing have always fascinated me.

I applied to one Seven Sisters school, to Duke, the University of North Carolina, and the University of Florida. Everyone took me except Radcliffe. I couldn't believe it. My board scores were so high they looked like pinball scores. My grade point average was 3.8. I should have applied to Smith. Well, too late. I took the University of Florida offer plus the scholarships they loaded on me. Twelve hours on bad roads (old Route 441) was the distance from Gainesville to Fort Lauderdale. I would bum rides with upperclassmen who had cars to go home on long holidays, because I wanted to be near Mother after Dad died. I liked college, I loved my sorority, Delta Delta Delta, but underneath I felt bad about leaving my mother. She pushed me away. She would not allow herself to be dependent upon me. She lived through her darkness alone. I was starting life and Mother was ending hers, so she said. What happened was that she overcame her grief and lived two decades after Dad's death. She was a happy woman. (As it turned out I supported my mother from the time I was twenty-two to her death when I was thirty-eight. This really made her happy!)

After my freshman year I came home to work during the summer. Mom was better—better enough so that we could fight. I am embarrassed to admit that I fought with my mother. I think it takes five years to truly recover from a profound loss, and by the summer of 1963, Dad had been dead only two years. Anyway, I thought I knew everything. Mother didn't give bugfuck about literature and I didn't give bugfuck about anything else. She didn't discourage me from being a writer; it's just that she herself was much more interested in visual arts. Mom liked her color. If she said "apples," I said "bananas." As I recall I wrote a lot of poetry at that time about cruel mothers. If the situation were reversed I think I would be writing about foolish daughters.

A black cloud appeared on the campus of the University of Florida in 1964 and attached itself to my head. I became involved in the struggle for civil rights. It was one thing to fight for civil rights if you were black. It was quite another to do it if you were white. The black individual was in danger but had a great deal to gain. The white individual was in danger and had a great deal to lose, namely the friendship of other whites. I also lost my scholarship over this when the school accused me of something I didn't do. Those sons of bitches weren't going to say this was due to my civil rights involvement. Still make me mad? How could you tell? Let me lay down to you Brown's law: Every American, regardless of race, class, age, sex, religion, or sexual preference, has a right to equal employment and the benefit of equality under the law. Many folks in 1964 were not interested in Brown's law nor in the great struggle to fulfill our own Bill of Rights. Christ, I've never been in so much trouble in my life, plus getting beat up for it. The violence was easier to take than the hypocrisy.

And that's how I found myself in New York City at age nineteen in the summer of 1964. No money. No nothing. But the theater was there. New York University, Washington Square campus, took me and I could get free theater tickets. If I couldn't get a free ticket I would go in after the first act and find an empty seat. The ticket takers didn't care. For three years I saw every show on and off Broadway, and since I often missed the first act, I had to reconstruct it. That proved useful later when I had to build plots. What was also useful was that I would write down what I had seen from my reconstructed first act and send it to Mom. Because she wasn't "literary," her responses to these stories were invaluable. She always found the holes.

You might think that New York would be a haven for a writer. I found it closer to hell. After the lavish colors and smells of the subtropics, the city was cold, gray, and overwhelmingly ugly. No wonder Yankees are so mean.

I lived in that monochromatic environment for ten years sustained by the Metropolitan Museum of Art and the theater. I grew to appreciate Manhattan's uniqueness, and someday, perhaps, I'll be rich enough to have a *pied-à terre* there.

A megalopolis is a magnet for writers but I don't think you can learn much talking to other people struggling at the same level as yourself and it's difficult to make contact with successful writers. I make it a point to avoid other writers except in rare circumstances. It isn't that I don't like them. I do. But shoptalk takes time away from the typewriter. You don't talk books; you write them, and the temptation among other writers is to talk yourself out. Actually, I don't talk about my work to anyone. Put up or shut up. I put up.

At age twenty-five I bought my first Mont Blanc Diplomat fountain pen. It cost $40. I mention this because that pen, to me, was the symbol and the tool of a real writer. Not only do I still have that pen, I have others in my bathroom, living room, bedroom, and purse. I love them. I want one within arm's reach no matter where I am. If I live to be a mean old lady I will have dozens. I also learned that the pen is mightier than the sword but the sword is easier to clean.

Soon after buying my magical pen I began to write my first novel. This was 1971. Prior to that date I had published many political articles in the underground papers (since dried up, which is a terrible loss for beginning writers) and I had published two books of poetry. My first book, *The Hand that Cradles The Rock,* was published by New York University Press when I was twenty-two. It is now out of print.

I wanted my novel to be so witty that even Republicans would be forced to enjoy it. I think my reach exceeded my grasp—it still does—but *Rubyfruit Jungle* was an energetic beginning. Daughters Press published it in 1973 after every major hardcover house in New York turned it down. (Eat your hearts out. You all had your chance.) There was no publicity. Not one piddling ad. The book sold 70,000 copies. It was like a prairie fire. Bantam Books bought it from Daughters Press in 1977 and the book has sold millions of copies. It is published in every major language in the world, although it is not sold in Communist nations.

What made me the happiest about my first novel was the fan mail. People wrote the kindest things to me. Every now and then I'd get a poisonous letter but I was amazed that anyone would take the time to be ugly. It's flattery in reverse. A critic is paid to be ugly. For a normal human being to put all that venom on paper is remarkable.

*Rubyfruit Jungle* taught me an important lesson: Seriousness is the refuge of the shallow. There are events and personal experiences that call forth seriousness but they are fewer than most of us think. The success of my first novel encouraged me to be wary of the conventional and to follow my heart.

About this time I also learned that a theme must come from within you. If it doesn't, you're nothing more than a hired gun. You won't be writing true fiction. It may be fictional in form but it won't be fictional in intent. This is no slam on being a hired gun. Sometimes you have to do it. Rent has a strange way of coming due on the first of the month. But true fiction is always lived from within and deeply felt.

*Rubyfruit Jungle* was followed by *In Her Day*, also published by Daughters Press and now out of print. This novel was a technical improvement on *Rubyfruit* but a commercial disappointment. In the theater and in publishing, a smashing first success is typically followed up by a bomb or a slender success. I was no exception to this rule. The book paid its printing costs and that's about it. I learned that obviously political themes replete with political arguments don't go down with American readers. For a variety of reasons, none of which I understand, our people shy away from political novels. They'll read a political thriller (helps if it's a spy thriller) and that's it. (The only exception to this rule that I know is Gore Vidal.) I wasn't daunted by the lukewarm reception to *In Her Day*. I was plain thrilled because I had jumped the Grand Canyon between first-person narrative and third-person narrative. After *In Her Day*, I knew I would gradually grow in strength until I could handle a main plot and as many subplots as my powers could carry. In fact, each novel I have written has been more complicated than the last, although on the surface the language is fairly simple. You'd be surprised how hard it is to be simple.

It must sound odd to you, rejoicing in a book that never hit the charts, that earned me $5,000 and that was it. But *Rubyfruit* only earned me $1,000 initially, so the money was never as important to me as the development of skill. Money, much as I enjoy it, will never provide the drive to my life. My drive comes from throwing my work out to you like a great beachball and hoping that you will play with it.

*In Her Day* was written immediately after *Rubyfruit*. By 1974, I was desperate to begin my third novel but I had no money. I used to buy old cars and fix them up and sell them, find antiques (e.g., mercury-center doorknobs) in houses about to be destroyed and sell them to dealers. I was just miserable. I needed time and I needed money. Try to remember back to that time. Very showy novels were the rage and they were quite often first-person narratives. Stories from a woman who was Southern, poor, and rebellious were not in big demand. I had an even worse strike against me: I was funny. Humor comes from self-confidence. There's an aggressive element to wit. It's one thing for a man to be funny on the page. Mark Twain was lionized for it (although for years people didn't realize he was writing for adults). It's another thing for a woman to be funny on the page. Erma Bombeck is screamingly funny but she's also on safe "feminine" territory. This is no criticism of her; I'm appreciative of her consummate skill. But I was not on "feminine" territory. From the very beginning I was bucking for my chance to hit in the majors. I took on the individual versus society. I invaded sacred male territory: war. I took on the power imbalance between women and men without apologizing to either men or women. Why? I am an equal opportunity offender. This combination of qualities guaranteed I would not be given a teaching position within the university even though I have my Ph.D. I would not be selected for special honors. I would most definitely not be on the Literary Mafia gift list.

I was working eight hours a day and then I'd come home and try to write for four hours. I was dead tired and I tried to save money by eating one meal a day. I figured I would put away what I saved until I had enough to quit my job for three months. Strange to tell, Yankees came to my rescue. The Massachusetts Council of the Arts granted me a small yearly stipend and with that amazing gift (I almost cried when I read the notice and I'm not a crier) I began *Six of One*. Halfway through it and nearly out of money I received another pleasant shock. The National Endowment for the Arts gave me a fiction grant. I finished *Six of One*.

Do whatever you can for the agency in your state that helps artists, and please, please, write your congressperson and senator to support and extend the programs of the National Endowment for the Arts.

Bantam bought *Rubyfruit* from Daughters Press in 1977. I finished *Six of One* in 1977 and Harper & Row bought it. Bantam Books could not make an offer because it was strictly a reprint house at that time. Now it brings out books in both hardcover and paper. When Harper & Row bought *Six of One*, I immediately set to work on the next novel, *Southern Discomfort*.

I was sharpening my Mont Blanc. I knew from my first novel never to introduce characters by telling everything about them. That's like giving the reader a heavy suitcase to lug for the rest of the novel. Show; don't tell. I was getting better at this because I was now learning how to use my environment both as another

character in the book and as a counterpoint to the human characters. I was halfway there with *Six of One* on that lesson, but by the
time I finished *Southern Discomfort*, I had it.

Each novel—with the single exception of *Sudden Death*,
which was written as a promise to a dying friend—was more
difficult than the previous novel. Interwoven, by this time, with my
novels were my screenplays and teleplays.

Like most everyone else, I started at the bottom. I don't mind
that a bit. The first movie I wrote was a spoof of horror movies
called *Sleepless Nights*. It was shot three years after it was written,
the send-up quality expelled, and lots more guts and gore added. It
was retitled *Slumber Party Massacre*, and it made Roger Corman a
tidy bundle. It made me $13,500. But I learned how to live without
narrative and how to rely on the image. (I'm still learning.) Every
time I finished a Hollywood job, I would come back to my novel
with a much more refined sense of the beauty and power of a novel.
This is not to say I can realize that beauty and power, only that I
appreciate it and I'm trying my best.

This period of my work coincided with the sorrows that come
to us all in time. I lost the love of my life, who unfortunately went
to the press about it. Public humiliation is a special torture. My one
consolation was that I kept my mouth shut and I prayed the day
would come when this would be behind me and we would be
friends again. Fortunately, the day did come. At this same time,
1981, I lost my money. When the two of us were together it never
occurred to me to keep what I earned for myself. I put it in a
common pot, the house. As my partner made much more than I
did, it seemed unimportant. Forced to put the house up for sale
(divorce is savage; first you lose your love, then you lose your
second seat of security—your house—and maybe you'll lose the
car, the dishes, etc., too), I was literally ruined when my Other Half
broke the contract after I had found a buyer for the house. I was
thirty-six, broke, and in a daze. I couldn't even run the house,
which was once again in my lap. I had to close it up and go to
California, where I took a job with Norman Lear. (Bless you,

Norman.) I received an Emmy nomination for that show, *I Love Liberty*, along with Norman Lear, Rick Mitz, Arthur Seidelman, and Richard Alfieri. I don't even know how I got to work in the morning. But I did. It was my first television show and I sponged up whatever I could learn. (Mostly, I learned to scale down.) After that was over, I came back to Charlottesville to pick up the pieces. Baby Jesus, my cat of seventeen and a half years, died the day after I came home, October 13, 1982. I knew Mother was next. Don't ask me how. She was the picture of health but I knew. Mother died on August 13, 1983. In a span of a year and a half I lost my past and I thought I lost my future.

But the English language was mine forever. Nobody could take that away from me. My work was my lifeline—that and my friends.

I never knew I could love anyone as much as I loved my ex-partner. I never knew I could miss anyone as much as I missed my mother. But Fate wasn't done with me. When I was eighteen, I was engaged to one of the most infuriating, exciting men I'd ever met. We grew apart in the romantic sense even as we grew closer spiritually and emotionally. We kept an apartment together in New York which we gave up when I was thirty-one. Jerry Pfeiffer contracted AIDS. None of us is quite sure how. He never said. He died September 14, 1985.

At the end of this period of my life, which lasted four years from start to finish, I didn't know whether I was coming or going. I had Mother's hospital bills and funeral expenses to pay and on top of that I was battered by the IRS because an accountant of years ago lost my Subchapter S form. (It's all very technical and confusing until they slap you for so much money you think you're going to the poorhouse. I really would like to keep the fruits of my labors and I wonder how much longer I and other Americans are going to put up with this.)

And yet, I loved my work. I was now up to my ears in research for what became *High Hearts*. I would get up in the morning and sometimes just cry, and as I said, I'm not a crier, but the pain of these losses was difficult to contain. I'd have my tea, turn on the typewriter, and the cats and dogs would come into the room. The work continued to seduce me.

I reread Livy in preparation for my work on our Civil War (the war of Northern Aggression, according to Grandma). I reread Herodotus and Thucydides. I fell in love with Greek and Latin authors all over again. And my long grim battle was over. Events around me became less lethal. I still miss those I loved who are no longer with me but I find I am grateful for having loved them. The gratitude has finally conquered the loss.

It was now 1986 and I realized that if I kept my health I would enjoy perhaps twenty-five years of peak performance. This doesn't mean that the public will retain an interest in me or my work for twenty-five years. It means that I know that's how much time I have left to work at this white-hot temperature. The knowledge that I would never be young again startled me. It didn't depress me—just woke me up.

I did what I usually do when faced with a revelation. I laughed. I understood that I wanted to laugh even louder. So I returned to *Six of One,* which has a structural peculiarity (I played around with time) yet overflows with a slap-happy, absurd dash in the face of Life. I wrote that as a young woman. I want to touch the same kind of joy but with the depth of middle age behind it. I'm working on that novel now and it's tentatively called *Bingo.* I am aspiring to be silly. If you ever read Aristophanes you know there are moments of such sublime silliness in his plays that you shout at the sheer pleasure of being so assaulted. That's what I want to do. I probably won't get there but it's a goal worth a life's work.

It's 1987. I am still not suffering from Affluenza but I make enough to live in a visually interesting house (I crave beauty) and I always have enough to eat. Considering where I came from, this is heaven. But paradise is the work itself. The process of writing, any form of creativity, is a power intensifying life.

The odyssey of any life surprises the sailor/seeker. It's so

easy, looking back from the security of middle age, to find dramatic
turning points. It reads better that way. But the truth of my life as
an artist is that I was and still am being built the same way a coral
reef is built. Millions of tiny microscopic creatures fall through
glistening waters to land upon the ocean floor. Eventually enough
of them fall to create a fanciful, habitable coral reef. The shapes of
these reefs are fantastic and they provide refuge and sustenance
for other creatures. So it is with this writer's life. The minutes have
fallen until my life has a definite architecture. To pretend that I
planned these minutes is a shout of egotism beyond even my
rather sturdy self-regard. I planned the Latin. I planned the reading. I wrote until my fingers ached. But I never planned the
humans that walked into my life. I never planned the historical
events that shook me: assassinations; betrayals of our sacred
Constitution by U.S. Presidents; the senseless slaughter of my
generation in the heat of Viet Nam; the extraordinary emergence of
a young, brainy Russian leader; the continued battering, both legal
and physical, of women and nonwhites. Those events I live with
and fight, just as my ancestors took in stride or stumbled at what
the Fates threw at their feet. Historical events are counterbalanced
by the joys of personal life, yet even those are out of my control:
the love of friends, the wonder of observing children becoming
responsible adults, the loyalty of animals, and the richness of
nature as well as the richness of creative life. What may be the
secret of being a writer is that you remember and utilize these
"falling moments," finding in them your themes, your contradictions (any good work must have opposing forces), and your emerging
order. Other people recall memories. You recall patterns on as
many levels as you are capable of: emotional, political, sexual,
spiritual.

Every time my coral reef becomes more beautiful or my game,
if you like sports metaphors, is raised to a new level of play, I am
as amazed as my supporters and detractors. I don't know how it's
going to turn out. What I know is that I have been given an
opportunity to work. I love the work.

When you think of photosynthesis versus writing for a living, photosynthesis is much more efficient. However, since I belong to the animal kingdom I can't convert sunlight into food, so I am trying to convert human experience into sunlight. I think of laughter as sunlight. Creativity is the animal kingdom's answer to photosynthesis. We take what is around us and make something new, something nurturing.

If you are a writer or you wish to become a writer you will have a different starting place than I had. Also, you may be spared having to reveal yourself in this fashion because you won't have your publisher telling you to do it. Actually, she was right. The progress of one person in a profession is usually illustrative to the progress of others.

If you are a writer—I will be blunt here—you should be writing novels, poetry, plays, or short stories. You should not be writing screenplays and teleplays under the misguided conception that they are literature. They are not. There's a chapter on those forms later. A screenplay may be beautifully written but it is not literature. The reason for this is simple. A work of literature must be the artistic expression of *one, unified consciousness.* A screenplay or a teleplay is never that. It is a cooperative venture or, sometimes, an uncooperative venture. It may be genius. It is still not literature. Even if you are very good at screenplays and teleplays, if you want to push yourself to the limit, you've got to work part of the year or part of your life with novels, poetry, plays, or short stories. That's the only way you get your spurs and your gray hair.

In my youth I was grape juice; now I'm fermenting. Ask me about how I developed as a writer even five years from now and I'm certain my emphasis will be different from what has gone into this first chapter. But now that I have fulfilled this responsibility to my publisher, we can get to the good stuff: you, the work itself, and some odds and ends.

I would like to close this chapter with something I think every writer should engrave on his/her wrist. Somerset Maugham said, "There are three rules for writing a novel. Unfortunately, no one knows what they are."

Truer words were never written.

# II

# YOU

# THE BEGINNING
# OF
# ALL LITERATURE:
# YOUR BODY

———

A writer's life is not designed to reassure your mother. The least you can do for yourself is take care of your body.

Art is presented as something that happens from the neck up. But creativity is not an isolated mental process. Your body is involved. You're working when you're writing, and work means sweat. The muscle effort isn't as obvious as for an athlete. However, the concentration on your task is so total that your muscles must obey as well as your mind. The better your physical condition the easier it is to write. That doesn't mean if you're a great athlete you'll be a great writer. What it means is that if you have the natural talent for writing, whatever discipline you expend on your body will affect your artistic output. You'll work better.

Writing is your Centre Court, your World Series. How curious that no one has paid much attention to the physical conditioning of artists in general, and writers in particular.

Much of what I have to tell you about your body is common sense. You need to eat properly and get enough sleep. If you're working at an outside job to support yourself while writing, something's got to give. Don't let it be sleep. Give up your social life. If you aren't prepared to put your writing first, you aren't really a writer. If you want to succeed, you've got to organize your priorities. Sleeping is more important than partying. For you to be successful, sacrifices must be made. It's better that they are made by others but failing that, you'll have to make them yourself.

Once you're on a regular sleep pattern you will discover that at some times of the day you are more creative than at other times. For me, this occurs about two hours after I'm awake. Everyone is different. The ideal for a writer is being able to organize your day around your best work time. However, if you're stuck in a nine-to-five job, you can't do that, so you have to learn how to crank yourself back up when you get to the typewriter.

One way to push up your output is through food. You can devour a lot of diet books and cookbooks. Forget them. Listen to your body. Your body will tell you when you need to eat and what you should eat. The problem is that we've arranged our day according to the dictates of labor or social life. Few of us eat when we need to. We wait for a designated lunch hour or we hang on until eight o'clock when we meet the Joneses at a restaurant. Learn to be unsocial. When you're hungry, eat, and always eat a big breakfast. If you're on the job, carry some apricots, nuts, or other non-junk foods. Snack a little. When you finish at your money job, come home and exercise if possible. Then eat something that's a good mix of carbohydrates and protein. Even if you have a dinner date, eat a meal when you need it. If your body says six o'clock, then six it is—to hell with fashion. When you get to the restaurant, just eat a light salad. If your friends don't like it, get new friends. You must be in good condition in order to create. If you were in training for the Olympics they'd understand. You are. Never let anyone or any social attitude stand in the way of your productivity.

If you're using sugar as a pickup, your body is giving you a signal. If you crave sugar, go to your doctor and get a glucose tolerance test. It's a real bore but the test doesn't hurt—it's simply time-consuming. You might be diabetic or hypoglycemic. If you are, this sugar imbalance will make you less productive.

Anyone reading this can get loony from sugar. Even if you aren't diabetic or hypoglycemic you can do damage to yourself. It's difficult to cut out every bit of refined sugar from your diet and I'm not suggesting that. I'm suggesting you watch it. For maximum efficiency of the whole body, the amount of glucose in the blood must balance with the amount of blood oxygen. Your brain registers this balance or imbalance immediately. As the most sensitive organ in your body, your brain reacts to the sugar long before your muscles do. How you feel—up, down, calm, or climbing the walls—depends in large measure upon what you're eating. Remember what happens to you when you drink too many cups of coffee? A constant overconsumption of sugar makes caffeine seem almost benign.

If you're a person without an inborn glucose problem, you can manufacture one. You're working hard on a novel. You aren't taking the time to prepare good meals. You don't have time anyway because of your job and if you've got children you're fighting for every second. It's late at night. You're tired but you want to keep working. You hit the chocolate chip cookies. Within minutes you feel a surge of energy and you work your tail off. Soon, maybe within a half hour, you feel exhausted, depressed, and irritable. More chocolate chip cookies. What's happening to you is this: Up until the sudden influx of refined sugar your adrenal glands were keeping your body chemistry running with the precision of a Mercedes. You got tired because you'd used up whatever you'd eaten for dinner. You became less imaginative and eventually your muscles became tired too. Remember that the brain gets priority inside your body and the brain will rob muscles of energy in order to function. That's when your muscles get tired—that and when you use them in heavy activity, of course.

But when you started to sink over the page, you ate those cookies. Refined sugar, sucrose, is the next step to becoming glucose. Sucrose passes right into your intestines, where it becomes predigested glucose. When this is absorbed into your bloodstream, there's trouble. The natural glucose level has already been established in your blood. You are now pushing over that natural level. Even though you temporarily felt great after those cookies, you put your body in a crisis. When this surge of energy was over, it was succeeded by the bottom dropping out of your blood glucose level. That's the pits. You can actually produce hallucinations by screwing around with your glucose level. The temptation to administer more sugar to your system is strong but to get the boost you want, you must keep administering the substance over and over again. In effect, you keep your body in a state of crisis. Add alcohol or drugs to that and you've got real trouble.

This doesn't mean you can't eat ice cream or enjoy your birthday cake. It means watch yourself. If you're loading up on the refined sugar, you need to drop back. If you can't, then go to the doctor. A blood sugar problem can lead to other diseases. Catch it now.

If you want to lose weight, don't do it while you're working on a major project. Writing a first draft of a novel puts your body under stress. Why compound the stress? Start your diet a week after you finish that first draft. If you want to lose weight I can tell you how to do it. My plan won't make any diet book. In fact it obviates diet books, but it works. The no-fail method is: You put everything on your plate that you normally eat; then take your knife and remove half of everything. This keeps you from gorging. Those fad diets deny you nutrients which you replenish the second you go off the diet. Back come the pounds. I call this my half-assed diet, since you'll lose half your ass. Better yet, it will stay off.

When I'm working on a major project I need to be at my fighting weight. This is five pounds less than my normal weight. It takes a lean hound for a long race, and novels and screenplays are long races. I feel better a bit underweight; I concentrate better and for some reason I am able to stand the back strain—a professional hazard—more easily. Your rhomboidei, the muscles up around your neck, tend to hurt when you work at a typewriter for hours. The small of your back can hurt too. Being a little underweight won't stop the pain but for me it minimizes it.

You can write a chapter on one hard-boiled egg and a cup of tea. That's efficiency. Figure on taking a break every two hours to drink milk, tea, or just to stretch your body. You'll get tense and you need to do what you can to give your muscles a break. One thing you can do is to lie flat on your back on the floor and bring one knee up to your chest, count to seven, then release it. Repeat the procedure for the other knee. There are many stretching exercises that will help you considerably. Rather than try to explain them on the page, I suggest you attend an aerobics class. Even if you don't want to hop in place while wearing pink tights and purple leg warmers, go to one good aerobics class. The stretching exercises will be so clear to you that you can go home and repeat them as needed.

Every four or five hours, depending on your stomach, eat a true meal. Relax for half an hour after the meal and then go back to work. You'll get much more work out of yourself if you do this. Those pages will pile up next to your typewriter. Seeing that accomplishment pushes you to write more.

Exercise will make you more productive. You've probably got a favorite sport. Do it. The problem with many sports is that they are time-consuming. Team sports become nearly impossible once you're out of college. That leaves tennis, squash, golf, horseback riding, jogging, fencing, handball, swimming, or even walking. If you're on a deadline, going over to the stables is impossible. It takes half an hour to clean and tack up the horse, more if he's muddy. You ride for an hour and then you've got half an hour to cool off the animal, wash him if it's hot, and clean your tack. I mention this because I love riding but when I'm on a killer deadline I must abandon it. No matter what your favorite sport, learn to exercise at home.

I've got a ten-station Universal weight system in my basement. I bought it over a decade ago. I like pumping iron. I can bench press 207, which is the max on my Universal system. I may get old but I won't get weak! The reason I love weight lifting is that I can leave the typewriter, go to the basement and work out for an hour, feel fabulous and come back to the typewriter ready for more hours of high-level work. Immediately after a workout I can write double time for about an hour. I don't know if this will be the same for you. But whatever you do—aerobics, rowing, handball—try to get to the typewriter right afterward to see if the activity has increased your creativity. You might be one of those people who needs to exercise after the day's work is done. When I'm on a more relaxed deadline I go riding. It's my reward for the day's work.

# GUZZLING AND SNORTING

Alcohol is associated with writers. The list of famous literary drunks could fill pages. Most of them are male but there are enough females to make one worry. Boozing is an occupational hazard for the male writer. What a pity masculinity wasn't defined as having a forty-two-inch chest instead of the ability to wench and hold liquor. Why Anglo-Saxon culture persists in this crackbrained idea, I don't know. Don't think you're off the hook if you're black or Italian. If you're an American citizen, Anglo-Saxon culture has permeated your system. Only if you recognize it can you retain the good points and fight the bad. Alcoholism is a cultural epidemic.

Today there is such an emphasis on health that young male writers might be able to avoid the Hemingway or Faulkner path. It's worth a minute to consider why writing is so hard on men and why booze soothes the wounds.

Have you ever heard a father say to his son: "Go be a writer, my boy"? Chances are if the young man strikes off for the arts, Dad is horrified. Has he spawned a fairy? Art in our country is perceived as a feminine activity. No one is going to walk up to you and say outright that literature and the arts are feminine, yet the assumption percolates beneath the surface of consciousness. Art concerns itself with emotions, and in Anglo-Saxon life, emotions are the province of women. Men are warriors. Women are prophets and storytellers. Go back and read *Beowulf* and our early literary efforts. The men in those tales are killers, fighters, action people. Granted, that is characteristic of the times, but the same ideals are with us today in slightly muted form. What do we make of men who seek to excel in female territory? We accept them only if they overtly deny their sensitivity. Hemingway liked to be photographed as a big-game hunter. He was so excessively butch that he was a caricature except to other men also nervous about their masculinity. It is not my aim to disparage Ernest Hemingway but rather to point out the lengths to which this gifted, feeling man went in order to prove he was "one of the boys."

I know I'm simplifying the case but the relationship of American men to the arts is sad, savage, and often hilarious. A European man doesn't have to pound his hairy chest and say, "Hey, I'm male. I fuck women. I can drink you sons of bitches under the table." All our European counterpart has to do is produce high-quality work. His masculinity is not jeopardized unless he shaves his legs. The European man will be praised for his skill, for his commitment and sacrifice to his art. He may even be elected to his nation's cultural academy, which formalizes the esteem in which he is held.

This mature view of the arts and a man's place in the arts is slowly dawning on Americans. I say "slowly" as in "Slowly the Ice Age ended." So if you are reading this and you are male, you have my sympathy up to a point. If you can't live your life without the approval of other men who haven't got your talent, I pity you. Since when is the opinion of cretins important, even if they do have money?

What fractures me about most men is that they can't live without male approval. Women can approve of them devoutly. It doesn't count. What the boys think is all that matters. Brother, I can't help you there. Either you learn to go it alone or you, too, start having your picture taken with dead giraffes and tigers.

Am I saying that literature is easier for women? Yes. It's easier to get into; it's not easier to be taken seriously. One of the ways men get revenge for being treated as quasi-homosexuals is to ignore or rip apart the work of women. If men are treated like second-class citizens, women are going to be treated like shit. Not every literary male behaves in this fashion but enough of them do to make your life, shall we say, interesting, if you're female.

The great advantage of being a woman writer is that no one will accuse you of sleeping your way to the top. In our business that's impossible. You live or die on the page.

If you're female and gay, watch out. You'll get one of two responses. You'll be told you write like a man. This is supposed to be a compliment but what they're really telling you, aside from the fact that men's work is more important than women's work, is that a lesbian is half a man. I don't know about you, sister, but that one really tears my ass with boredom. The other response you get, and I confess this is my favorite, is that you are a man-hater. No one will say that directly. What they'll say is that you can't create satisfying male characters? Has Norman Mailer ever created a believable female character? I think he's written some extraordinary books but they don't connect with female consciousness, and as far as I'm concerned, that's okay. He's giving us what he can and that's a hell of a lot better than what many others are doing.

So if you are a lesbian, be prepared. They'll take you seriously as an artist when you're dead. Then you can join the ranks of the angels like Stein, Cather, and Colette.

The response to gay male writers is perhaps the saddest of all. Heterosexual men don't even bother with a facade. They go straight for the throat. They've spent their lives denying they are gay and then here comes a homosexual who can write with beauty, truth, and power. Small wonder Tennessee Williams and Truman Capote devastated themselves with alcohol. Small wonder, too, that many gay male writers stay in the closet. Often those who come out write only of gay life, as though gay people do not live with and around heterosexuals. You can argue that heterosexual writers rarely create good gay characters. I agree. However, the gay writer grew up straight. The gay writer knows two cultures. The straight writer knows only one. The gay writer ought to be able to create more diversified worlds. The straight writer certainly can choose to create diversified worlds but he or she must learn to pass in reverse, if you will. The more you know about people, the better you'll be as a writer. Whites need to learn about blacks, Chicanos, Asian-Americans, and so on. Men need to learn about women, and straights need to learn about gays. Maybe those lives will never appear in your work but you will be informed, broadened, and deepened by learning from others.

Getting back to gay male writers. If you happen to be one, you have one choice and one choice only: You've got to be better than anyone else. For what it's worth, I'm on your side. I delight in talent magnified by pressure. Show me a writer, any writer, who hasn't suffered and I'll show you someone who writes in pastels as opposed to primary colors.

I got started on all this because I don't want writers to drink. Let me tell you a few things about alcohol. No, I'm not going to tell you; I'm going to hit you over the head. If you seek solace or inspiration in the bottle, you're an asshole.

Alcohol blasts you quickly. It's chemically akin to glucose and ether. Both act quickly on your brain but can't be stored. Alcohol supplies heat energy but no nutrition whatsoever. It contains no vitamins or amino acids. These are required for the metabolism of alcohol, so there is a constant nutritional disorder in chronic alcoholics. For many people alcohol depresses the appetite, so instead of answering the body's need for food, they drink more. The body becomes narcotized by booze. Even in young people the deterioration and loss of reflex speed is rapid. By the mid-thirties one's appearance is altered negatively.

Alcohol is metabolized at the rate of ten to twenty milligrams per hour, depending on your height, weight and sex. If you could drink an ounce of whiskey in the course of an hour, you'd stay sober. But compulsive drinkers knock back several drinks within an hour. It's like drinking napalm. Sooner or later you'll burn away your creativity.

In order to write at a high level of competence you need a comprehensive vocabulary, a keen sense of overall structure, and an inner beat or cadence. Your senses must be razor-sharp. Alcohol blunts those senses even as it releases self-restraint. Therefore many writers feel they are getting down to the real story after a belt or two, little realizing they are damaging their ability to tell the real story. There's got to be another way to release inhibition. For me it comes through exercise.

Worse, alcohol causes memory distortion. The substance literally alters your brain, so not only is your memory distorted but you also lose insight and your personality changes. These factors cause most drinkers to deny that they are dependent on the substance. Alcohol is an allergy of the body and an obsession of the mind.

I'm not saying you refuse a drink at a social occasion—provided alcoholism doesn't run in your family. If it does, why start in the first place? That's like playing Russian roulette. What I'm saying is that an enjoyable vodka tonic on a Sunday afternoon isn't the same as two belts of Jack Daniel's before you start work.

Please be honest with yourself about drinking. Yes, it will hurt your work. It will hurt you and it will hurt the people you love. If you have problems with the stuff, go to Alcoholics Anonymous. It's one of the places that can help you and it doesn't cost you anything.

Drugs, to date, lack the allure for writers that liquor holds. After the War Between the States, drug addiction shot up because it was the only answer for those veterans suffering chronic pain. They had morphine, and by the 1880's they had cocaine. But drugs didn't intrude into the national consciousness until the wild 1920's. Even then they were a habit of the very poor or, in the case of cocaine, a habit of the very rich. By the 1960's drugs had "progressed" to that vast population, the middle class. Also, there were new "designer" drugs cooked up in chemistry labs at the universities.

The real reason that cocaine is sold is so that Americans will convert to the metric system. I feel the same way about drugs as I do about drink. If you want to do it socially, that's your business. The problem is so few people can stop there.

The only merciful thing about drug abuse is the speed with which it devastates you. Alcoholics can take decades to destroy themselves and everyone they touch. The drug addict can accomplish this in a year or two. Of course, suicide is even more efficient.

Take care of your body. With health you can produce into your eighties; this is the tremendous advantage of being a writer. You can never be put out to pasture. Think of Colette, G. B. Shaw, Rebecca West, or, among the living, Marguerite Yourcenar, Eudora Welty, Iris Murdoch, Robert Penn Warren, May Sarton, Muriel Spark, Anthony Burgess, Robert Heinlein, James Michener, Malcolm Cowley, Robertson Davies, Harriet Doerr, Saul Bellow, and Jorge Luis Borges. You get better and better as you grow older. It's the joy of the art.

# SEX, LOVE, AND ROCK 'N ROLL

―

This chapter will be blunt. You might not like what follows but it's based on my life experience as well as observing other writers.

Sex. How can you create characters if you yourself are sexually rigid? I suppose you can lock yourself into characters similar to yourself. After a few books, you may not be bored but your readers will be.

As I write this, Americans are reeling into a state of neo-Puritanism, a natural reaction to the excesses of the late sixties. Today, this fear of sexual contact is real. Concern over AIDS is not neo-Puritanism; it's self-preservation. My purpose here is not to demean the legitimate concerns of the right wing. I share their worries. My solutions to the problems are different from their solutions. So is the fact that I respect them. They apparently respect no one who does not agree with them. Much of this battle is over sex.

Sex is a natural act. Nothing is unnatural, only untried. If you're going to write about passion, you'd better feel it. Now some clever soul reading this is going to say, "Well, if you're going to write about murder, then you have to murder." No, you do not but you have to *understand* murder. That means you reach deep down inside and call upon your own murderous impulses. If you have none, let me show you the way to Calvary. You're in a class by yourself.

You don't have to put a yellow *yield* sign over your bed. If you do, that's your business and for your sake I hope you're careful. But you need to know a lot about physical responses and, more, how those responses, apparently biological, have emotional repercussions for most of us.

Virginia Woolf said that writers must be androgynous. I'll go a step further. You must be bisexual. If you can't carry out the act, again, that's up to you; you'd better get as close as you can imaginatively. You must create men who love women and women who love men or your books will be lopsided. In the beginning of everyone's work the dice are always loaded toward one's own sex or sex preference. Learning to unload those dice, to throw the bones honestly, is what maturity as an individual and as a writer is all about.

Americans fall far behind Europeans when it comes to identifying with the opposite sex. It shows in our literature and it showed early with James Fenimore Cooper. He created stories of almost mystical bonding between his white hero and his male Indian companion. The women were cardboard figures. Herman Melville went Cooper one better. He put men on a ship so there wouldn't be any women at all. Even Twain, a remarkably advanced thinker concerning women, did not create a fully developed female character. At least he created likable minor ones; that was an advance, culturally.

Americans are struggling to reach out, to embrace our sexual opposites. Oh, we can do it in bed but we're having one hell of a time doing it on the page.

If you consider how sexually rigid we are, the fact that few lesbian or homosexual characters show up in the novels of overtly heterosexual writers makes sense. Hell, they can't even identify with their wives or husbands, much less somebody still further away from them.

It's a terrible weakness. There are ways to overcome it without jumping on everyone. Of course, the other ways may not be as much fun. Obviously you need to expand your circle of friends to include as many different kinds of people as possible. Observe them. If they'll talk about their sexual/love experiences, listen. Do not judge. Never presume to judge another human being anyway. That's up to heaven.

Some people tell all. Take advantage of it. Those who don't tell all tell more than they know. Everything you learn will be helpful.

Sexual knowledge continues throughout your life. You ought to know more at forty than you did at thirty. I'm not talking about technique but about the impact sex has upon your health, your outlook, your expectations.

Love, while often allied to sex, exists on a separate plane. You can love someone and never sleep with that person. But let's confine ourselves to the mixture of sex and love we seem to be looking for in our private lives. So that I won't be misunderstood, let me say this: Monogamy is contrary to nature but necessary for the greater social good. You're on your own with that one.

Some writers find sex energizing. They hop out of bed and roar at the typewriter. Everyone finds out what works for her/him.

What doesn't work is a love relationship in conflict with your work. This will happen more often than you think. Writers exert a mysterious pull upon the average person. Do people have visions of serving Art? Of inspiring *War and Peace*? Do they dream of dedication pages emblazoned with their names? Whatever, being a writer means you'll attract more than your fair share of lovelies. Great. Just wait. The initial attraction wears thin when Ms. X or Mr. Y discovers what hard work writing is. Oh, at first they are understanding. After a while they resent the time you're spending at the typewriter, and when you aren't at the typewriter you're dreaming about a scene, a character, a good line. Most people prefer that you be dreaming about them. It must be killing for a person to say "What are you thinking about, dear?" and instead of hearing "I'm thinking about how beautiful you are," to be told, "I was thinking about how the passive voice destroys responsibility. It removes the agent of action." It takes a very unusual woman or man to live with and love a writer.

If upon meeting someone for the first time s/he suffers a burst of enthusiasm when s/he discovers you're a writer, be suspicious. If s/he wants to read a work in progress, be really suspicious. Nobody has the right to ask that. You can grant someone the right to read your work as you write it but no one should ask.

What a writer looks for in a relationship should be peace. Most of us can't write in chaos unless we were weaned at the city desk on a metropolitan newspaper. One can have peace and passion. They are not mutually exclusive.

You need someone who can be supportive without being intrusive. You also need someone who can be supportive without being a doormat. The doormats will destroy you faster than the tyrants. You'll die of guilt and boredom.

How lovely if your mate loves literature but how unnecessary. What's necessary is that your mate love you.

Never expect your partner to understand your work. You can hope that he or she appreciates it, but don't push your luck. Hell, *you* might not even understand your work. Think of it this way: You're married to a neurosurgeon. Does she ask you to come into the operating room with her? Does she laboriously explain her craft to you? Don't burden anyone, including another writer, with your trials at the typewriter. It's unfair.

This applies to parents also. Why should they understand you? It would be nice if they did, since they are responsible for bringing you into this world, but never underestimate the power of self-absorption, including your parents' self-absorption. Much as they may love you, they probably aren't that interested in your sufferings at the keyboard. If you are reading this and you're still young, still living at home, and your parents actively discourage you from writing: Forgive them and get out the minute you graduate from high school. It's hard enough to write without other people setting up roadblocks.

The other problem with parents is that once you do produce a book, they are either furious that you've misrepresented them or furious that they aren't in there in the first place. Egos are never hidden. They can be easily reached with an insult. Unless you portray Mom and Dad as walking saints you're in deep doodoo. This anger takes a year or two to dissipate. If the book is a success and makes money, the anger dissipates much faster.

Which reminds me. If you write a book and there's a tempestuous relationship in it, get ready for your lover/wife/husband to be nettled. One hopes that one's partner is beyond that and can realize that fiction is experience plus something magical. They get the experience. They don't always get the magical. They'll become hardened to it after you produce more books.

Friends respond in much the same way as one's parents or spouse, only the reaction is less intense, usually. I once had a friend in a full fury because I named a dog after her. My reply was that if she'd treated me better I would have made her the Queen of England. She got the point.

Children. Few things you do in this life demand as much responsibility, steady income, or emotional maturity as raising children. Despite feminism, this task still falls on women more than on men. I made a choice not to have children although I love them deeply. I knew I could not take care of two kids and write novels. Why two? Well, you can run after two and catch them. Add that third one and I knew I'd be constantly exhausted. I also knew that my husband or lover, if I was with a woman, probably wouldn't take care of the children so I could lock myself up and write. Men should be confronted with the choice, too, but since they can foist the kids off on the wife, many a male writer blithely reproduces and finds out too late that he's a rotten father. Some of you can have kids, be you male or female, and do your duty by them. Many of you cannot. Don't fool yourself. Sit down and think of what you need to write and how much money you need to live. Can you afford a full-time babysitter or *au pair*? If not, can you afford the guilt of knowing your mate is doing more than her/his share (if s/he is)?

Can you afford the doctor's bills, the dentist's bills, etc., etc.? Above all, are you emotionally prepared to tie yourself to a twenty-four-hour-a-day job for eighteen years? Children need you. It's not an equal relationship. You give more than you get from children. Can you do that? The reward is knowing that you have that much to give to another human being. I have no doubt that genuinely loving your children, providing for them, teaching them right from wrong, and enjoying each stage of their development, add up to one of the most fabulous experiences of life. *But* don't do it if you can't fully give of yourself.

Whether you have children or not, you can learn a great deal from them. The way children learn language is a gift to a writer. First they learn nouns and a few simple verbs like *go* in the present tense. Then come more present-tense verbs—other tenses do not come until much later because verbs are a sophisticated concept. After the bone and the muscle are grasped, they begin to use adjectives and then adverbs, subordinate clauses, and so on. It's a fascinating process. Recognition of function always precedes recognition of being.

I have read Piaget's books concerning children but I can't say that I have well researched the subject of how children learn language. What I have written here is based on my own observations. I think your observations are probably as good as mine and I wonder if your findings will concur with my own.

Apart from language, children teach you the basics in human psychology. Every emotion and every defense shine on their faces until they learn to hide their feelings. You must become a child when you write. You must find that sense of wonder, that sense of newness, while maintaining your adult level of skill and philosophy.

Rock 'n roll is what you do after you're finished with the day's creative output. I'm good creatively for four to five hours. After that, it's a case of diminishing returns. I've learned to stop. If you're at all like me, whatever your peak duration of work, you have to decompress. I can barely carry on a conversation. The head wanders and the body is exhausted. What I do is go riding or throw rock 'n roll on the stereo and move around a little. The only way I can come back to normal life is to do something physical. I take great pains to avoid people during this decompression period. That's why horses prove boon companions. They have no desire to talk to you. I need a good hour to restore myself.

Some of you may be able to leap away from the typewriter and chatter with the brilliance of Noel Coward. More power to you. Most of us will decompress one way or another. Here again is where drugs and drink can be seductive. You're keyed up. Your rhomboid and deltoid muscles hurt. Your jaw is tense. Since you're a slave of the lamp, your eyes burn. The temptation is to decompress with a shot or a toot. Don't do it. You must teach yourself to respond physically. If you don't want to blast Aretha and dance, then jog or do yoga, weed your garden or play with the cats. My point is, the solution to the state you're in is physical.

# THE
# IVORY TOWER
# AND THE
# CITY DESK

Education is a wonderful thing. If you couldn't sign your name you'd have to pay cash. A university education is a process of acculturation. You learn discipline—more if you study Latin than any other subject—and you learn how to use the library as well as resource people. The university exists for many reasons, not the least of which is to keep young adults off the streets for four years. One acquires there the minimum skills for a decent job in the labor force. How much education you need beyond your undergraduate days depends on your field and your ambition. Yours truly has her Doctor of Philosophy. I can honestly tell you it hasn't done me a bit of good.

Universities are nurseries of orthodoxy. The university, while often a nurturing environment, is not a creative one. It can't be. That isn't the function of higher education. Think of it this way: The university is dedicated to a nonfiction view of the world, a scholarly approach to life. If you're a fiction writer, a playwright, a poet, or any kind of creative artist as opposed to re-creative artist, you're in the wrong place. A creative artist makes something new. Literally creates. You are a synthesizer. A re-creative artist takes what you have done and refines it or presents it to the public. An actor, director, or editor is a re-creative artist. The composer is the giant. The conductor is the hired help, no matter how brilliant. Does that make the definition clear? The university can't even assist the re-creative artist. It's poison to the creative one.

Flannery O'Connor said, "Everywhere I go I'm asked if I think the university stifles writers. My opinion is they don't stifle enough of them." Funny as this quote is, it doesn't mean you should not attend college. You need access to the experience of others. Knowledge is cumulative. That is reason enough to get your Bachelor of Arts. Also, the more you know about the mainstream of our culture the better off you are. If you are going to break with that mainstream, you have to know exactly what you are breaking from. To put it another way: You can't be truly rude until you understand good manners.

There's a blueprint for a writer's conservatory at the end of this manual. This would be a place where writers could develop their technical skills, much like a music conservatory. This is not to be considered in lieu of the university but as a postgraduate program.

Yes, I'm telling you to put yourself in a noncreative environment for four years. You need the background, you need the scope, and you need to meet other people involved in the same process. Nothing you learn, no matter how silly it may seem at the time, will ever be wasted on you. Writers *use* everything. Tell yourself that in the middle of a calculus exam.

The bitterness of so many writers toward the university makes the place sound like pestilential society. These writers sit under an apple tree and beg it to drop a pear. The university not only is not a safe haven for writers, it will eventually vitiate your work. Get in, sister and brother, and then get out.

You will have to withstand the vagaries of professors. Most academicians love what they do. A few, and unfortunately you usually find them in writing departments or other "creative" departments, do not. This is brutal but you've heard it before: "Those who can, do. Those who can't, teach."

If one loves to teach, if one is a midwife to literature, then lacking creative talent is compensated for by developing it in others. However, some people are so angry at their lack of creative success that they fill their students full of bile and bunk. How many times have I talked to young writers, fresh from a university course, worrying about compromising their talent by "selling" it. Of course these students hear this line from a disgruntled professor. Since he can't make it in the real world, he's going to tear apart everyone who does. Don't ever fall for that bullshit. Envy is a belittling emotion. Better a tarnished genius than a simon-pure hack.

You need to test yourself in the outside world. Your life, your labor, your time are worth money. A writer should be paid for her/his work and paid well.

Let another writer tell you about money and your work. Colette was asked by Arthème Fayard to write an article for the magazine *Les Nouvelles Littéraires*. He told her she could name her price. She did and he was astonished. He said, "But Gide asks a quarter of that for an article." Colette replied sharply, "Gide is wrong. If that is the way famous writers behave, what happens to the ones who are hungry?"[1]

Another problem with the university is the narrowness of its environment. For four years that narrowness is good, because you focus on your studies, learn to socialize more effectively with your generation as well as with some older people, and you have athletic equipment right there under your nose. So many young writers, fearing their ability to earn a living and continue writing, think if they go to graduate school and then teach afterward, they'll have more time. You don't. If you're a teaching aide or you get your Ph.D. and start on the bottom rung in an English department, you'll stagger under the workload. You earn the right to work less as you get older in the university. Perhaps "work less" is the wrong choice of words. You earn the right to specialize.

The siren call of the university is the two- or three-month vacation. You can write at that time. Summer vacation is the best thing about staying inside the academic world.

[1]Claude Chauviere, *Colette* (Paris: Firmin-Didot, 1931), p. 878.

It takes as long to learn writing skills as it does to become a neurosurgeon. This society constructed an apprentice system for the neurosurgeon. It has built nothing for the writer. Cruel, yes. Effective, also yes. Our system separates the wheat from the chaff. Go out into the cruel world.

One alternative chosen by many writers is journalism. This is a much better choice than hanging around the university. For one thing, you are actively writing even if you aren't writing about a subject dear to your heart. In a way it's better, in the beginning, not to be writing about something so close to you. You get defensive and can't correct yourself or take correction. Okay, maybe you're the exception. Most fledgling writers can't take hard editing. Journalism short-circuits that process. You have to produce or you hit the pavement. You have to snare the reader with the first line (called a "hooker" in our trade). You have to be clear, concise, and write good transitions so you can slide the reader from paragraph to paragraph. It doesn't much matter if you're writing about eggplants or hockey. The drill is the same.

Journalism, the mother to literature, will probably be a mother to you. I started out there. I've still got the bruises on my soul but how I learned!

You get paid for your work in journalism—not well, but paid nonetheless. This is much better than in the university, where you do not get paid for writing. (You have to publish, but a monograph on Yeats's use of the semicolon is hardly the same as a 3,500-word piece on the famine in Ethiopia.)

The competition is tough. You hustle or you starve. I was luckier than you will be because I came of age during the civil-rights and the antiwar movements. Underground papers covered the United States like kudzu. I was published very early. I didn't earn a dime but I got paid in copies which I could then take to another paper to land another job. Eventually I broke into overground magazines and sold an article here or there. That paid enough to buy cat food. Can't write without a cat.

Today that vine of protest has dried up. Now you go directly to the overground press. Most cities have a big newspaper and a small one, a kind of anemic weekly. Start at the bottom. There are 12,242 newspapers. One of them is bound to take you. There are also 22,238 magazines. If you get a column or an assignment from that four-page weekly, grab it. You've got to get your name in print. You might have to struggle for a few years at this level but if you can write clean prose you stand a chance.

In the meantime you work at what you can. I used to paint houses. The result is you can't pay me to paint a damn door now. Ugh. I also used to sand floors. I found that physical labor kept my mind cleaner than if, say, I'd worked for an advertising firm. Physical labor is still the province of men. If you're a woman, about all I can say is do a good job. Even if they resent you on the construction site they will eventually respect a good job. The other thing is—shut up. It isn't worth fighting with some bimbo who is threatened by a physically competent woman. Save your fire for the page. My experience working in all-male environments is that the average man is fair. Don't be soured by the flaming assholes of this world. I've found the same thing working in all-female environments, with one exception (you can argue about this all you like): Women are more cooperative with one another. It's easier to concentrate, initially, on the task, because you don't have to dance through the ego pecking-order ritual.

Don't burden people on the job with the fascinating news that you are a writer. For one thing they don't give a shit. For another thing it sounds as though you are trying to be better than they are. You aren't better. Different, not better.

So far, journalism looks like a great thing and it is—up to a point. Nobody can tell you when you'll stumble over that point but you'll feel it. It's simple, really. A fiction writer is a fiction writer. S/he is not an academician, a critic, a nonfiction writer, a journalist, a screenwriter, a poet, or a playwright. A fiction writer may write any of those things if s/he is versatile, but fiction writing is analogous to nothing but itself. That means journalism really is your mother. You've got to be weaned.

If you've been offered a terrific editorship from a magazine that pays great, the choice is difficult. Only you know when you've absorbed enough to go. Only you know if you've saved enough money, and most of us can't because we don't get paid enough in the first place. But go you must. City rooms and publishing houses are filled with people who say, "I coulda been a contender." Don't be one of them. There are many reasons for failure but no excuses. You've got to cut the cord.

You can only go back to journalism or the university after you've made your way in the world. That takes decades. And if you're still vital and still getting work, chances are you'll not return. Remember them fondly even if you left in anger: They got you where you are now.

# COMPUTERS AND OTHER EXPENSIVE KNICKKNACKS

---

What you need as equipment is a sharp pencil and a piece of paper. This modesty of expense is glorious, since so few writers make money from writing.

Naturally, the salesman at the local computer store will tell you that his product will do everything but come up with plots for you. What can a computer do? Not much more than a typewriter when it comes to your first draft. Where a computer helps you is on every draft after that. Revisions are miraculous with these machines. You can dump paragraphs, delete words, move sections of prose around like a pinball flying in the machine. That saves time. The drawback is it takes time to learn to use the computer. I don't care how many books tell you it's easy—it still takes time. Even when you think you know what you're doing, you can wipe out a day's work.

If you get a computer it has to produce decent type. Publishers are prejudiced against manuscripts that are hard on their eyes—unfair but true.

The cost of computers varies considerably, much like the cost of automobiles. Radio Shack sells a Model 100 for $399. At least that's the price here in Charlottesville, Virginia in the spring of 1987. There's a Tandy 1000, single drive, 128K for $710. The IBM PC, with two drives and a monitor, sells for $1,925. My researcher, Claudia Garthwaite, uses our AT&T 6300 personal computer with a

Hewlett-Packard LaserJet printer and Hayes Smartcom II modem. The whole shebang cost me $5,412.16. It was worth every penny. The software we use is Microsoft Word and that retails for $365.

Does this mean I compose at the computer? Not a chance. I need to hear the clack-clack of the typewriter and I dearly love yanking a splattered page off the roller. A computer removes these intense satisfactions from my day. I work at an IBM Correcting Selectric III. Once I've knocked out a first draft, I hand it over to Claudia. The rewrites go on the computer.

As it is, I still haven't bought a terminal for myself. I probably never will. Mary Lee Settle, one of my favorite writers, used to write by hand on enormous sheets of paper. The physical act of writing and the sensuality of the paper appealed to her. Ms. Settle did break down and buy a computer but many writers can't. Switching to a different mode of production inhibits their work. For some writers, the deliberateness of writing by hand forces them to choose their vocabulary more carefully.

My work involves mountains of research. Claudia puts much of the information on the computer. What's great about that is we've cut down on the clutter in the office. There are still towering piles of books on the floor and on most available surfaces but we can move about. Before the computer we needed a compass to find our way through the books.

The other good thing is that Claudia can put the phone to the computer, and a machine on the other end will type out the pages. Sometimes screenplay deadlines are fierce and that feature is terrific.

You can also do much of your own day-by-day accounting work. I find if I have to go over the bills I spend less than if I have bills routed to my accountant's office. It took me years before I could afford an accountant and when I did it took me years to become accustomed to having one. (If you can do your own taxes, congratulations. Taxes are so complicated they have spawned a huge professional class to deal with them—which may be the point.) Doing monthly bookkeeping saves me about $300 a month, oftentimes more. Obviously, you need to take your materials to your accountant each quarter, but you'll save money by using an accounting package for daily life.

A good typewriter is more essential than a computer, and why spend money on a computer if you haven't got much money in the first place? Besides, why take the time to use a computer? That's what children are for. They know more than we do anyway.

A new IBM Correcting Selectric III costs $945. A reconditioned one is between $500 and $700 but they're hard to get. IBM's new Wheelwriter has a memory capacity which provides a computerlike function with the feel of a typewriter. The cost is approximately $100 more than the Selectric III. They don't make IBM Selectric II anymore but you can get a reconditioned one for about $400 to $600. The replacement for that model is the IBM Actionwriter. The reason I stick to the IBM product is not because salesmen here know what they're doing but because I think the product is superior to anything else in the marketplace. I've used Smith-Coronas, Olivettis, old Underwoods and Royals, but IBM is the easiest typewriter to use if you're pounding away hour after hour. The funny thing about IBM is that the company is so big they don't even canvass writers to find out what we need or have to say. I don't know if it's arrogance or ignorance on their part, but the true devotees of their equipment are not secretaries but scribblers.

The IBM service contract is sound and I've had very good luck with service people. They know what they're doing. The other thing about IBM is that they offer, once or twice a year, sales on ribbon and correcting tape. I buy in bulk and get a savings. I am always informed ahead of time by mail that one of these discount sales is coming up and I appreciate that. It helps me prepare my budget.

You need good light. I spend hundreds of dollars on lighting in my workroom whenever I move. Right now I work with spotlights, five, at 150 watts each, on a track over my head. Behind me, running like an L, are six more 150-watt spots and immediately over the typewriter is one of those fancy Italian lights that looks as though it belongs on a flying saucer. My late friend and first publisher, June Arnold, could work only in a basement room with one naked light bulb swaying overhead. June wore Coke-bottle glasses but she swore it had nothing to do with her lighting peculiarities. Don't skimp here. You're better off with expensive lighting than a computer. Those damn computers hurt your eyes, too. As occupational hazards go, you might as well know now— your eyes are going to fade. It's inevitable. You strain them daily in this kind of work. I started life with 20-15 vision. That's better than 20-20. My profession has taken its toll and I'm becoming more nearsighted with each year.

You probably think that's why Milton went blind. I think he went blind so he wouldn't have to read any more unsolicited manuscripts.

You need a good dictionary. Make that a great dictionary. The price of the *Oxford English Dictionary*, thirteen volumes, is $900. When I bought my set they cost about $600. There is an *OED* compact edition with magnifying glass that sells for $175. You can't place a value on the *OED*. Even if you must pay it off over time, *do* buy the thirteen volumes the minute you can afford it without going hungry. You will never regret this purchase and you will use it until the day you die—after which time your children and grandchildren will use it. Be aware, however, that *OED* spellings are British, e.g. theatre instead of theater.

You can get *Webster's Third New International Dictionary* for $80. It's better than nothing.

The following is a list of basic reference materials which you would be wise to consider. Prices quoted are at 1987 rates.

*The Basic Book of Synonyms and Antonyms*, paperback (New York: New American Library, 1986). $2.95.
*Concise Oxford Dictionary of Quotations*, 2nd ed., paperback (London: Oxford University Press, 1981). $8.95.
Patrick Hanks and Flavia Hodges, *Dictionary of Surnames* (London: Oxford University Press, 1986). $75.
J. A. Cuddon, *Dictionary of Literary Terms*, paperback (New York: Penguin, 1982). $8.95.

*Roget's II: The New Thesaurus,* paperback (New York: Berkley, 1985). $3.95.

*The World Almanac and Book of Facts* (New York: World Almanac Publisher, published annually). $5.95.

William Strunk, Jr., and E. B. White, *The Elements of Style,* 3rd ed., paperback (New York: Macmillan, 1979). $3.50.

Stuart Berg Flexner, *Listening to America: An Illustrated History of Words and Phrases from Our Lively and Splendid Past* (New York: Simon & Schuster, Touchstone Books, 1984). $13.95.

These books are not as vital but you may find them useful.

Jacques Barzun, *Simple and Direct: A Rhetoric for Writers,* paperback (New York: Harper & Row, 1984). $6.95.

Hallie Burnett and Whit Burnett, *Fiction Writer's Handbook,* paperback (New York: Harper & Row, 1979). $5.95.

Curtis W. Casewit, *Freelance Writing: Advice from the Pros,* paperback (New York: Macmillan, 1985). $8.95.

Becky Willliams, ed., *Writer's Market* (Cincinnati: Writer's Digest Books, published annually). $21.95.

H. W. and F. G. Fowler, *The King's English,* paperback (London: Oxford University Press, 1985). $6.95.

Jean M. Fredette, *Fiction Writer's Market* (Cincinnati: Writer's Digest Books, published annually). $18.95.

*Literary Market Place* (New York: Bowker, issued annually).

*New American Desk Encyclopedia,* paperback (New York: Signet, 1984). $5.95.

William Safire, *On Language,* paperback (New York: Avon, 1981). $6.95.

Lastly, you need one cat, although two are better. Cats keep you from taking yourself too seriously. They also are good judges of literature. If a cat won't sit on a freshly typed page it's not worth much. Think of your cat as the original Muse.

# III
# THE WORK

# WORDS AS
# SEPARATE UNITS
# OF
# CONSCIOUSNESS

---

Language is the road map of a culture. It tells you where its people come from and where they are going. A study of the English language reveals a dramatic history and an astonishing versatility. It is the language of survivors, of conquerors, of laughter.

A writer must have a philosophy of language as well as a philosophy of life. You need to know how English works.

The sensible place to start is with individual words. A word leaves a smoke trail behind it that curls into the past. Every word is surrounded by complex energies. There are meanings underneath a word as well as its obvious meaning.

Think of a word as a pendulum instead of a fixed entity. A word can sweep by your ear and by its very sound suggest hidden meanings, preconscious association. Listen to these words: blood, tranquil, democracy. You know what they mean literally but you have associations with those words that are cultural, as well as your own personal associations.

Let's take one word to illustrate my point of meaning in flux: Revolution. *Revolution* enters English in the fourteenth century from the French via Latin. At least that's when it was written. It may have been spoken earlier. *Revolution* means a turning around. That was how it was used. Most often *revolution* was used by astronomers to indicate a planet revolving in space. The word carried no political meaning.

The word *rebellion* was the loaded political word. It, too, comes from Latin (as does about 60 percent of our word pool) and *rebellion* means a renewal of war. In the fourteenth century, *rebellion* was used to indicate a resistance to lawful authority. This can yield amusing results. Whichever side won the "rebellion" called the losers rebels; they, the winners, being the repositories of virtue and more gunpowder. This meaning lingers today. The Confederate fighters are called rebels. Since the North won that war, it can be dismissed as a rebellion and not a revolution. Whoever wins the war redefines the language.

*Revolution* did not acquire a political meaning in English until the sixteenth century, when it meant a circular movement. It's still tied to its origin but has now spilled over into politics. It can mean a turnaround in power. This is more complicated than you might think.

The sixteenth century, vibrant, cruel, progressive, held as a persistant popular image the Wheel of Fortune. If you've ever played with a Tarot deck you've seen the Wheel of Fortune. Human beings dangle on a giant wheel. Some are on the bottom turning upward, some are on the top, and some are hurtling toward the ground. It's as good an image as any for the sudden twists and turns of Fate, Life, or the Human Condition. This idea was so dominant at the time that the word *revolution* absorbed its meaning. Instead of a card or a complicated explanation of the Wheel of Fortune, one word, *revolution*, captured the concept. It's a concept we would do well to remember.

Politically, *rebellion* was still the more potent word. As late as 1640, Cromwell's seizure of state power was called the Great Rebellion. (Remember, Charles II followed Cromwell in a restoration of monarchy—hence, Great Rebellion. Cromwell didn't call his actions "rebellion.") In 1688, when William and Mary took over the throne of England, the event was tagged the Glorious Revolution. *Revolution* is benign here and politically inferior in intensity to *rebellion*.

By 1796 a shift had occurred and *revolution* had come to mean the subversion or overthrow of tyrants. Rebellion, specifically, was a subversion of the laws. Revolution was personal; it was directed against a living individual. So we had the American Revolution, which dumped George III out of the colonies, and the French Revolution, which gave us the murder of Louis XVI and the spectacle of a nation devouring itself. If you're a Marxist you can recast that to mean one class destroying another. At any rate, the French Revolution was a bloodbath, and *revolution* began to get a bad name as far as monarchists were concerned and holy significance as far as Jacobins were concerned.

It was during the French Revolution that *revolution* developed into the word we know today. *Revolution* now meant not just the overthrow of a tyrant but a belief in a new principle. Revolution became a political idea, not just a political act.

The Russian Revolution, the Chinese Revolution, the Cuban Revolution—by now, *revolution* is the powerful word, not *rebellion*. In the late 1960's and early 1970's, young Americans used the word *revolution* indiscriminately. True, they wanted political power, they were opposed to a tyrant, and they believed in a new political principle (or an old one, depending on your outlook): participatory democracy. However, that period of unrest with its attendant creativity did not produce a revolution. The word quickly became corrupted until by the middle 1970's, *revolution* was a word used to sell pantyhose.

Whither thou goest, Revolution?

You, by now, should understand that words are separate units of consciousness. As a writer you must know something about the history of your language and its word pool. Or as Mark Twain said, "The difference between the right word and the almost right word is the difference between lightning and lightning-bug."

Tinkering with individual words is always a good exercise. Change "Your Honor" to "Your Virtue." How about Hollywood to Hollyweird, or administration to administrivia? Once you understand a word you can fiddle with its insides or substitute another meaning. If you're sensitive to words you can create humor in this fashion. The English language reeks with comic potential.

Play with words. Take similar words or ones in which there are shades of difference. For instance, what's the difference between involvement and commitment? Think of ham and eggs. The chicken is involved. The pig is committed. See what I mean?

# THE
# TWO ENGLISH
# LANGUAGES

Fortunately for the English writer we possess the largest vocabulary in the world. The base of this ocean of discourse is really two rivers flowing together: Anglo-Saxon and Latin.

English is the second-largest language in the world, spoken by 358 million. Mandarin is first, with an estimated 650 million speakers and Russian is third at 233 million speakers.[1] Since both Mandarin and Russian are politically compromised as artistic instruments of expression, that leaves English as the world's most important literary language. English has conquered the world. Let's hope you will conquer with it. Apart from our freedom of speech, our language itself is fluid. We "learn" quickly. This openness is barely apparent in Anglo-Saxon with its limited vocabulary. The fortunes of war altered English forever.

Until 1066 we did fine with what we had. When Harold fell at Hastings, shot through the eye with an arrow, our language was overwhelmed by Norman French. We now had High English and Low English. These divisions are with us to this very day and provide the subtle shadings of meaning available to a writer through careful word choice alone.

[1]David Wallechinsky, Irving Wallace, and Amy Wallace, *The Book of Lists* (New York: Bantam Books, 1977).

High English is Latin. Well, it's really Latin that came through French because the Normans spoke French. When the Normans took over, everything Anglo-Saxon was ruthlessly shoved aside. Culture was Latin. Granted the Romans invaded Britain in 53 B.C. and discovered what every tourist has discovered since: England is an aquarium, not a nation. The Romans managed to colonize us but it was superficial. The true intrusion into our native tongue did not occur until 1066. After that time the words for the enjoyment of life were Latin. The words for labor and games were Anglo-Saxon.

So if you were a lord and sat down to a feast you ate beef. The poor peasant tending what became your meal called it an ox. Calf when it hits the table becomes veal. Sheep becomes mutton, and swine becomes pork. Deer when eaten is venison, and boar is brawn. The division was clear and will be with us as long as English is spoken. The main reason the Anglo-Saxon words survived at all is because the native population was not killed but utilized as workers. The other reason for Anglo-Saxon's survival is that the people themselves proved more resilient, flexible, and intelligent than William and his progeny could have imagined. These qualities are reflected in the language itself and I'll get to that when I cover hybrid words. We are an exceedingly creative people, and I mean by "people" all those who speak English as their native language. You can be black, yellow, white, red, or brown, but if you grew up speaking English the language has been imprinted on your brain. You are, in a deep intellectual and creative sense, Anglo-Saxon/Latin. You will seek solutions to problems. Other languages, more conservative ones, accept the problems as given. You must begin to realize what a tremendous advantage this language gives you even if you live in political protest against the governments it has created.

When you create a character you can develop that character through her/his dialogue. An upper-class person will use a more Latinate word pool, more subordinate clauses, and longer, less volatile speech rhythms. A character from the lower classes will use more Anglo-Saxon words, much more colorful speech patterns, and shorter, staccato rhythms unless this character is from the American South. In that case, rich and poor alike are more prone to use the rhythm of the King James Version of the Bible. Here again, the poor character will employ more Anglo-Saxon words and will probably be more emotionally direct.

The intrusion of Latin gave us a reservoir of synonyms unlike anything else in the world. We abound in choices. Unless you are lazy or stupid you can find the precise word in English. These synonyms allow us shadings of class and meaning that can be textured, literally. They can be felt, not just heard.

This is a baby list of parallel words. When the Normans conquered the Anglo-Saxons these words had parallel meanings. As you go down the list you will see how the centuries have pulled apart the synonyms. Some still have equivalent meanings. Many don't. One could fill an entire book with such lists. I've plucked out common words. If you want to test your sense of touch, make sentences using the English word first and then substitute the Latin word.

| OLD ENGLISH/ANGLO-SAXON | LATIN/FRENCH |
| --- | --- |
| woman | female |
| happiness | felicity |
| hut | cottage |
| bill | beak |
| friendship | amity |
| dress | clothe |
| help | aid |
| folk | people |
| hearty | cordial |
| holy | saint |
| deep | profound |
| lonely | solitary |
| to give/to hand | to present/to deliver |
| darling | favorite |

| | |
|---|---|
| love | charity |
| begin | commence |
| hide | conceal |
| feed | nourish |
| hinder | prevent |
| look for | search |
| inner and outer | interior and exterior |
| leave | abandon |
| die | perish |
| mouth | oral |
| nose | nasal |
| eye | ocular |
| mind | mental |
| son | filial |
| house | domicile |
| book | literary |
| moon | lunar |
| sun | solar |
| star | stellar |
| town | urban |
| watery | aquatic |
| heavenly | celestial |
| earthy | terrestrial |
| timely | temporal |
| daily | diurnal |
| truthful | veracious |
| kingly | regal |
| youthful | juvenile |
| weighty | ponderous |
| share | portion |
| wretched | miserable |
| same | identical |
| murder/killing | homicide |
| manly | virile |
| kind | sort |

| | |
|---|---|
| tale | story |
| up | ascend |
| put out | extinguish |
| come near | approach |
| unlike | dissimilar |
| freedom | liberty |
| cold | frigid |
| sleeplessness | insomnia |
| half | semi |

Brief though this list is, it gives you an idea of the potential for nuance. Think, too, about deep emotion. If you've fallen through the ice you scream "Help!" You do not yell "Aid!" In times of greatest danger or heartbreak, even the most aristocratic of people will revert to Anglo-Saxon. As a writer, remember this, because it is the language of greatest emotive power.

It should be obvious to you that you must learn Latin. It's not a difficult language but, as in learning anything new, it takes time. Some universities offer crash courses, which means that within a summer you could master the basics of the language. Memorizing the vocabulary takes time but you know a lot of it anyway in its Anglicized form. You ought to learn enough Latin to be able to read Horace and Livy. Okay, Livy's kind of tough. How about Cicero? Anyone can learn to read Cicero. I'll be brutally frank: If you don't know Latin, you don't know English. If you want to write, you need this tool. Would you dream of becoming a neurosurgeon without a study of anatomy?

Some of you reading this are going to be upset. You think you're talented. You probably are, but talent is no substitute for intensive training. You can't sit down at a typewriter and write from your heart and expect it to pay. That's a little like saying "I love my child who is sick and because I love my child I will operate on her." Just because you feel something strongly doesn't mean you can translate it into a form accessible to a reader. You must be trained, and to be trained you must have discipline. Honey, if Latin doesn't give you discipline, give up. Once you've mastered Latin you not only know a great deal about English, you know how to think.

The other thing you must do—and do this only after you can read with some fluency in Latin (won't take you longer than two years, absolute tops)—is to take a course in Anglo-Saxon. You can fly through it, although the reading, in a funny way, is harder than the Latin. I think that's because we expect it to be familiar and it turns out to be just familiar enough to throw us off the track. But a semester of Anglo-Saxon will give you a great deal of information about our basic vocabulary and our original grammatical structure. It's terrific stuff.

If you already know Latin and Anglo-Saxon, bless you. If you've learned a modern language as well, praise be—you're way ahead of me. Scattered like jewels throughout both Latin and Anglo-Saxon are symbols, recurrent themes. I'll address symbol and myth later, but briefly, the apprehension of symbol will give you power as a writer. A symbol is a kind of literary landmine. Latin and Anglo-Saxon are treasures of these explosives.

If you aren't willing to study language, then you aren't willing to be a writer. Writing is honest labor and hard labor at that. You must be trained and you must be disciplined. One brilliant, isolated book does not a writer make. You go out there every day and you work. It's the difference between the fine country club tennis player and the one who wins Wimbledon. The one who wins Wimbledon works, perfects, struggles, and will play in a hurricane if she has to. The country club player does it when she feels like it. If you aren't willing to pay the price, don't bother coming out on the court.

# VERBS,
# OR
# PUT THE PEDAL
# TO THE METAL

―

Verbs blast you down the highway. If you want to get your black belt in boredom, load your sentences with variations of the verb *to be.* Granted, sometimes you can't help using them, especially with nonfiction, but at every opportunity knock out *is, are, was,* etc., and insert something hot.

Strong verbs are always hot. A strong verb changes forms inside the word itself. The sound alters. *Drink, drank, drunk* is a strong verb. *Love, loved, loved* is a weak verb. Strong verbs, memorized from childhood, spill off our tongues. Imagine how difficult it is for a non-English-speaking person to learn the language. We create past tense in two ways. The first way—as in *drink, drank, drunk*—and the second way—by adding "ed" to the ending—must drive the poor souls to evangelists or bourbon. If you're a native speaker you are hardly aware of this peculiarity. But you hear strong verbs differently from the way you hear weak verbs. As a writer you've got to hear them like separate notes on a scale.

I'm not saying that weak verbs lack punch—it depends on the sentence—but I am saying that the "to be" family falls flat on its face with overuse.

English is the international language of pilots. The language conveys maximum information in the minimum amount of time. Verbs help our ability to condense and transmit information and so does our sentence structure.

If you've studied Latin you know it's an inflected language. Endings, like earrings, hang on to words; they tell you the tense of the verb, whether a noun is a subject or direct object. In English, we've dispensed with inflection and we rely on word order. While our language is remarkably flexible, on this one plane English is rigid, immobile, unalterable. I can say "Man bites dog" in terms of word order in Latin and it still means the dog bites the man. *Virum morderet canis* or *Canis morderet virum*. It doesn't matter how I shift the words around, because *um* in *virum* means the man is the direct object of the dog's teeth. If I used *vir* then man would not be the direct object but the subject of the sentence.

An English speaker says, "The dog bites the man," and that's the end of it. While this locks us into structure it does give us speed. We know where our verb will appear. It's between the subject and the object. Yes, sometimes it can be at the beginning of the sentence when we command someone: "Come here." The subject, "You," is understood. And sometimes, for poetry's sake, it can appear at the end of the sentence but this is uncommon. Our verbs hinge our thoughts. It's literary architecture.

I studied Attic Greek in college. It nearly wiped me out. The sentences are built like onions. You peel away layer after layer, adjectives, modifiers, and so forth. So an adjective can be on the left side of the verb modifying a noun resting to the right of the verb. Finally, buried in the heart of this Godawful mess, is the verb. By the time I found it I was too exhausted to look at the ending and identify the tense. Furthermore, I no longer cared. To hell with Thucidides. I reached for the crib. This complicated structure gives Greek a facility with intellectual material that shimmers. The language dazzles but you've got to be patient. English speakers are not patient people.

You and I have only to stick our verb where it belongs and all is well. There are no surprises.

This quickness of our language forces us to choose words carefully. We need the exact right word to make up for our lack of inflection. No wonder we've got the largest vocabulary of the world's languages.

Therefore the verb is the key to writing. You know that your sentences can be slowed down with subordinate clauses. You can drop anchor by using passive voice—and if you aren't careful you'll drag your entire sentence down with that voice. You don't want to write at the same speed. You need to vary it and the way you do that is with your verbs.

Any action verb will accelerate a sentence. Run, jump, shoot, ride, and so on. However, if you've got characters sitting in a formal dining room, your verbs better reflect some inner motion or the reader will be bored by the characters' physical inactivity. So you might have a character steaming, seething, writhing.

My point is not that you hurtle the reader forward at every opportunity but that you be technically aware of how verbs control the movement of your prose. It's as easy to write a peaceful, light paragraph as it is to write a torrent. You choose when and where. Don't let the verbs choose for you.

Aside from providing the energy in a sentence, every verb is a clock. Coded into the word itself is the time of the action. So, present tense is exactly that. Unfortunately, a rash of novels in the last decade have been written in the present tense. It's a fad and it won't last. There are good reasons for writing in the past tense.

The first is familiarity. Every story we've read since *The Iliad* has been written in past tense. Don't argue with thousands of years of success.

The second reason is that the reader needs and wants distance and protection from the story. This safety zone, provided by the past tense, allows the reader eventually to open up for the emotional impact of the story. You've got to vault your reader's defenses. The reader doesn't want to get hurt, yet you want that reader to identify with your characters and that means to feel their pain and their joy. I feel strongly about this. Anyone who buys your book has plenty of problems in his or her life. You have no moral right to disturb them unless you also entertain them. Art is moral passion married to entertainment. Moral passion without entertainment is propaganda, and entertainment without moral passion is television. By using the past tense (except in your dialogue, of course) you enable your reader to come to you.

The third reason to use past tense is technical. Do you want the reader to focus on the story or focus on your participles and gerunds? Don't distract a reader with your style. That's you showing off. A great style is one that appears effortless and one that is individual. Your voice should not sound like Faulkner's.

The fourth reason to use the past tense and not the present tense is: Why would anyone want to read a novel that sounds like a screenplay? Screenplays are in the present tense. They have to be. You're giving the director his marching orders. Fiction is not a screenplay. A screenplay can be a work of towering imagination but it will never be a novel. The two functions are unrelated. There's a chapter on screenplays and teleplays later. I'm not disparaging screenplays. I've written seven of them and hope to write many more. I'm saying don't mix your mediums. It's trendy and you'll get attention for a while and then boom, it'll be over.

There is one good reason to write in the present tense and that is to gain immediacy. My feeling is you can capture immediacy through your dialogue. The sacrifices of tradition, reader identification, and technical smoothness don't justify the use of present tense.

Past tense is one thing. Past perfect is quite another. Why load auxiliary verbs? You're freighting down your sentence, and also, the cadence gets predictable and soon tedious. What's the purpose of *had* and *have* jammed in front of otherwise healthy verbs? Are they anemic? Are they lonesome? Do they need to feel that old familiar "to be" verb snuggled up against them? Get rid of that stuff. I use past perfect only to indicate a long passage of time. For instance. Simple past—"I was walking the dog" or "I walked the dog" (see, already you've got a choice; English forces you to make choices)—means you performed this function recently. If you say "I had walked the dog" or "I have been walking the dog," the time frame is different. You should be able to feel this difference. Time is a tool. You don't want to confuse your reader by confusing your time frames within your sentences. You might wish to check a grammar book. Sometimes by dropping the past perfect you will be committing a grammatical error. However, you will still be picking up reading "speed." It's a difficult choice. Unless something happened at a distinct point in the past or you wish to call attention to the event, consider laying off the past perfect. Then when you do use it, it will have impact. Your reader isn't going to be technically aware of what you've done but s/he'll sense the result. Never, ever underestimate your readers. Everything you do registers.

English is in a constant process of both simplifying itself and enriching itself. Since the past perfect means one more word to stack up, one more beat to slow one down, there is a possibility it will be used less in time.

So I'm trying to anticipate the future. This is tricky. First I excoriate authors who use the present tense but then I state my willingness to bend a tradition—nay, not a tradition, a grammatical law—to gain "cleanness."

I am aware of the contradiction . . . and I'm willing to brave it.

The last thing I have to say is that ice is the past tense of water. I've always wanted to write that sentence and now I have.

# THE
# PASSIVE VOICE,
# OR THE
# SECRET AGENT

Avoid the passive voice whenever possible. University term papers bleed with the passive voice. It seems to be the accepted style of Academia. Dump it.

The times you need to use the passive voice are as follows: 1. You don't know the active subject or you can't easily state that subject. Hence, "The store was robbed." 2. The subject is plainly evident from the context. 3. Tact or social delicacy prevents you from identifying the active subject. This also allows you or your character to pass the buck. 4. The passive connects one sentence with another. "She rose to sing and was listened to with enthusiasm by the crowd."

Deleted agents teach us how devious people can be. Let's look at a benign example: "The murderer was caught yesterday." Who caught him/her? Perhaps the writer doesn't know. On the other hand, perhaps the murderer is the writer's brother and she doesn't want you to know. Knock out the agent and you're fine until someone has the brains to question you.

Our government displays unusual genius in its official style. They have sanctified the deleted agent. Here are two ripe examples.

"Secret commitments to other nations *are* not *sensed* as

infringing on the treaty-making powers of the Senate, because they *are* not publicly *acknowledged.*"[1] (Italics mine.)

How about this one? "It was there thought best to commence with the addition of 25,000 regulars to the existing establishment of 10,000."[2]

Dear reader, tell me, who thought it best to add 25,000 regulars? Who decided on 25,000. Same person? Different people? Squadrons of people?

The use of deleted agents in government documents demonstrates vividly that language has a moral function. Language, supposedly, should tell us something. In these examples the opposite is true: Language is used to obscure. What is the difference then between the authors of the Pentagon Papers and the authors of Soviet documents? When a government seeks to evade responsibility, it no longer governs by consent; it governs by guile and possibly by the club. I am not suggesting that our government is analogous to the Soviet Union's. Let's just say that when it comes to accepting responsibility, both systems leave something to be desired. The irony of government duplicity via its choice of writing style is that removing the agents of responsibility contributes to making people feel powerless, alienated. They fall away from the system. Don't then turn around, Mr. Elected Official, and squeal and holler that voter turnout is low. Participation depends on a sense of responsibility. If government people are unwilling to take responsibility, why should the public?

Language exerts hidden power, like the moon on the tides. You can think, "Hell, so government documents are loaded with deleted agents. So what? You're making a big deal out of it because you're a writer, so you see writing as the basis for everything." Not exactly. I see language as the basis for civilization. Without language we couldn't form governments. We're doing a

[1]Neil Sheehan, Hedrick Smith, E.W. Kenworthy, and Fox Butterfield, *The Pentagon Papers* (New York: Bantam Books, 1971).
[2]Gaillard Hunt, ed., *The Writings of James Madison* (New York: G.P. Putnam's Sons, 1900).

piss-poor job of it with language but it's still better than being controlled by the physically strongest person in the tribe. The abuse and debasement of English in government documents has serious long-range consequences. It creates public cynicism and eventually encourages disrespect for the government and for law. You and I have a right to know who does what to whom, when, and where. If we don't start to demand that, we deserve what we get.

Another infamous trick with deleted agents is to appeal to the "generic person." Journalists do this a lot. You get this construction: "It is known" or "It is understood" or "It is thought." Who knows? Who understands? Who thinks? What's going on is a con job. The suppressed deleted agent is really "All right-thinking people know" or, closer to the truth, "All people who agree with me understand." You'd be surprised how often people fall for that because no one wants to be out in the cold. Agreeing with the speaker or writer means that you're "in the know."

Passive adjectives give you another opportunity to lie. They occur immediately before a noun. The agent can't show up in this type of construction, so an assertion can slip by unchallenged. Here's a good example: "Men regard as amusing this *exaggerated* fad of trying to substitute 'Ms.' for 'Mrs.'" 'Exaggerated by whom?

Nominalized passive provides us with yet another twist. Here a verb becomes a noun. So *refuse* now becomes *refusal; destroy/ destruction; enjoy/enjoyment; use/use,* and so on. You can obscure responsibility with the nominalized passive. "*Impoundment* of billions of dollars of allocated funds represents an unparalleled *seizure* of power by the White House." Who is impounding and seizing? Apparently the White House. How can a structure impound money? It looks as though we've been given an agent, but we've been duped. A house can't seize money. Yeah, well, it's the White House.

'For this and other examples, I am indebted to the pioneering work of Julia Penelope (Stanley), and in particular to her groundbreaking discussions of the passive voice in "The Stylistics of Beliefs" in *Teaching about Doublespeak,* edited by Daniel J. Dietrich (the National Council of Teachers, 1976) and "Passive Motivation" in *Foundations of Language* 13 (1975).

What does that mean? Does it mean the President? The agent of responsibility is halfway obscured. It could be the President but it could also be the downstairs maid. Does the President know what his minion has done? See what I mean?

In this example of using the nominalized passive, the agent isn't expressed at all: "What is needed is more intentional control, not less." Control by whom?

Experiencer deletion is one of my favorites. Putting this technique in the mouth of a gossipy character yields humorous or vituperative results. Politically, of course, it serves exactly the same function. What you do here is, you remove the person responsible for the perception. In most usage this perception is understood to belong to the speaker/writer. When the experiencer pronoun is stated it is usually a first-person pronoun.

"You seem to me to be getting careless." The speaker is taking responsibility for her/his perception. But "You seem to be getting careless" removes the perceiver. This implies that other people share this perception. What other people? The entire world knows you are careless. Mercy.

Try attributive adjectives. Those are *appropriate/inappropriate; proper, effective, acceptable, clear,* and the like. "The outlines of an effective technology are already clear." Clear and effective for whom? Imagine this sentence buried in a paper before your city's planning commission. The presenters of the paper want to tear down low-income housing and put up a high-rise for upper-middle-income people. Attributor adjectives seek to suppress the emotive element in any conflict and present information in a "scientific" manner.

When all else fails, why take responsibility? Try the flat-out lie. Here is my absolute favorite. When a reporter pointed out to Ron Ziegler, Nixon's press secretary, that Nixon's statements were considerably contradictory, Ziegler calmly stated before God and America that the President's previous statements were "inoperative."[1]

---

[1] *Facts on File,* Vol. 33, No. 1694 (April 15–21, 1973).

The passive voice, while grammatically useful, must be handled with care. Aside from the above usages of the passive, that voice can also signify a withdrawal from the world. Not feeling responsible is a form of withdrawal. If you want to think of it as grammatical existentialism, okay. Of course, I think when existentialism came over here from France it should have been packed right back to Paris. Let the French suffer with it. Americans have better things to do with their time.

A good example of passive voice being consciously used to illustrate withdrawal comes from Hemingway's *Old Man and the Sea*. (Another writer, Bertha Harris, brought it to my attention.) "He did not like to look at the fish anymore since he had *been mutilated*. When the fish had been *hit* it was as though he himself *were hit*." and " 'But man *is* not *made* for defeat,' " he said. " 'A man can be *destroyed* and not *defeated*.' " (Italics mine.)

Reading that passage makes me sad, not only because of what Hemingway is writing about but because such a talent belittled himself with his he-man charade. When you're as good as Hemingway, gender is irrelevant—informative but irrelevant.

Being alert to the passive voice makes you technically stronger. It also sharpens your senses for everyday life.

# HYBRIDS:
# THE ALCHEMY
# OF THE
# ENGLISH LANGUAGE

A hybrid is a composite word made up of two parts, the native language and a foreign language. Many languages have hybrids. Usually they borrow the foreign word wholesale and transform it somewhat into their own language. People make jokes about the Russian language and form hybrids without knowing the hybrid itself is the essence of the joke—i.e., computernick, peacenik. Here the foreign word is modified by the Russian ending. Even French, going through a period of ludicrous conservatism by "banishing" foreign words, contains hybrids. What makes English so different, so rare, is that we take a native stem and paste on a foreign ending. We've been doing this for centuries. It's a basic feature of our language and one of the reasons we are so surprisingly flexible. You can say anything in English if you think about it long enough and hard enough. You're about to see why.

Let's start with regular hybrids. Here you take a word, any word, be it foreign or native, and you tack on a native English ending.

---

### VERBAL NOUNS

-ing (more on this later)                          swimming

---

You've just doubled your vocabulary. Most verbs can be magically transformed into nouns. Aside from doubling your vocabulary it gives you a new cadence, something to play with and enjoy.

## SUPERLATIVES

| | |
|---|---|
| -est | noblest |

Superlatives probably amused you when you learned Latin because they sounded funny. A non-English speaker would find the *-est* sound equally funny. It is a way for you to raise the power of an adjective without adding on the freight of many qualifiers. For instance, if you couldn't use a superlative and you wanted to indicate that Catherine the Great was the most noble woman you could imagine, you might just say that or you might say very, very, very noble. Someone could come along and add a fourth very to the noble before Elizabeth I's name and she would then be more noble than Catherine. The issue is settled by *-est*. If you and your rival want to argue the virtues of your favorite queens (mine is Divine) you may do so without wasting time on qualifiers.

## PLAYING WITH NOUNS

| | |
|---|---|
| -ness | faintness |
| -ship | courtship |
| -dom | martyrdom |

This is a lot of fun. You have to memorize what native ending would go best with your chosen word but fiddling with that affords humor. *Martyrship* as opposed to *martyrdom* is funny and in the mouth of the right character will be funny to your reader too. Again, you can see the flexibility these endings give you.

## MAKING ADJECTIVES

| | |
|---|---|
| -less | artless |
| -ly | princely |
| -ful | beautiful |

You probably use these adjectives so often that you don't realize they are like an insect larva. This is the same creature—i.e., butterfly—that you are seeing in a metamorphosed state. Try to alert yourself to these changes the next time you read something. Again, the English vocabulary has expanded because of a native device.

## MAKING ADVERBS

| | |
|---|---|
| -ly | easily |

Perhaps you recall your fourth-grade English teacher hounding you about adverbs. Although children and adults use them and transform stem words into adverbs, they usually don't know that they're doing it. I don't know why but almost any linguistic activity involving verbs or adverbs seems harder to understand than nouns, or maybe it's just harder for me.

You can also turn a verb into a noun, and you have to do this when using the nominalized passive. So *refuse* becomes *refusal,* and *destroy* becomes *destruction.*

So far so good, and English is in line with other languages. They all need to make their vocabularies work harder for them. Here's where we shoot off in our own direction. You'll be amazed at how many foreign grammatical devices we have lifted when we add foreign endings to English words. English speakers don't seem to worry about linguistic purity. English speakers want results. If there's a way to say something faster, cleaner, and better,

even if it's Chinese, the English speaker will use it. If it's really
good it will quickly pass into the language. This adaptability
provides us with versatility. In a profound way, the English language pushes its users toward solving problems. Century after
century this language reflects the preoccupation of its speakers:
How can I do it better?

The English language does resist defining inner emotional
states and I'll get to that when I cover the subjunctive tense. What
we do better than anyone else in the world is solve problems that
are technical. English speakers like a visual result. As long as the
problem exists outside ourselves—e.g., How do I move thirty tons
of grain from Iowa to New York City?—we English speakers are
not only comfortable, we love it.

Here's how we do it.

---

### HYBRIDS WITH NATIVE STEMS AND FOREIGN ENDINGS

| | | |
|---|---|---|
| -ess | (to make a noun) | goddess |
| -ment | (to make a noun) | enlightenment |
| -age | (to make a noun) | acreage |
| -ance | (to make a noun) | hindrance |
| -ous | (to make an adjective) | murderous |
| -ry | (yet more nouns) | bakery |
| -ty | | oddity |
| -fy | (to make a verb, but fallen into disuse) | speechify |
| -fication | (noun from adjective) | uglification |
| -able | (most useful in forming | peaceable |
| | adjectives but you can | reasonable |
| | form verbs, usually | usable |
| | passive) | |
| -ability | (noun from verb) | drinkability |
| | | punishability |

---

It looks as though we trotted around picking up endings
wherever we went. We can also form adjectives by leaving out the

preposition. To the best of my limited linguistic knowledge, English is the only language to invent this. We use it all the time. For example, *indispensable* stands for "that which cannot be dispensed with." See the time we've saved? How about: accountable, objectionable, available, reliable? The list could cover entire chapters. Once again, English speakers came up with a way to make the language fly.

Here are some more endings. As a test for yourself, you figure out the function of the ending. Does it create a passive noun or an adjective or what?

|  | |  |
|---|---|---|
| -ee | | referee |
| -ive | | aggressive |
| -ible | | sensible |
| -ation | | starvation |
| -ist | (*ist* and *ite* are sometimes interchangeable) | Trotskyist |
| | | sophist |
| -ite | | Trotskyite |
| -ism | | witticism |
| -ocracy | | democracy |
| | (used as a joke) | drugocracy |
| -ology | | theology |
| -archy | | hierarchy |
| | (used as a joke) | catarchy |
| -ize | | womanize |
| -al | | maniacal |
| -en | (The following all make | silken |
| -ish | adjectives. Thought I'd | boyish |
| -y | give you a break so you | flowery |
| -ly | only have to figure out | motherly |
| -like | the preceding endings.) | doglike |
| -some | | toothsome |
| -ful | | sinful |
| -ine | (This stem is not | bovine |

(This stem is not English, nor are some of the above. Can you find them?)

Not only did we lift endings from other cultures we took prefixes as well. The following prefixes are Latin.

| | | |
|---|---|---|
| ex | (out of or former) | ex-king |
| | (now you know why) | Ex-Lax |
| anti | (against) | anti-pornography |
| pre | (earlier) | prewar |
| ante | (*before* is the English word) | antebellum |
| de | (especially used with *-ize* verbs) | desensitize |
| inter | (between, among) | intermingle |
| post | (*after* is the English word) | postwar |
| re | (again, to come back) | rebirth |

One more look at an ending and then we can press on: *-ing* (or *-ung,* which performs the same function). You probably use this ending more than any other because, over the centuries, it's been evolving until it's a workhorse. It does the following things for you.

In the beginnings of English, *-ing* could only be attached to a noun, so *school* became *schooling.*

Some of the nouns using *-ing* became a form of weak verbs. The ending began to be considered the verb. Then we started to apply this to regular weak verbs and we had a big time with it. A weak verb, as mentioned earlier, is one whose root word does not change when you change tense. Work, worked, worked. (People make jokes using the technique of strong verbs—i.e., think, thank, thunk.) Of course, for the purposes of sound, strong verbs are fabulous. Try *run, ran, run* or *sing, sang, sung.* But in order to learn faster and more easily, a weak verb is preferable. Being a practical people we mixed up our verbs. We even began to convert strong verbs (*crow, sprout*) into the weak verbs you use today. The peak of this conversion process happened before Shakespeare, or at the time when our people spoke Middle English. This drives non-English-speaking people mad because they want one rule to cover all our verbs. To them it's as though we have a raft of irregular verbs which must be set to heart. They aren't irregular. "To be" is irregular. Remember *sum esse fui* in Latin? Well, you can see why *speak, spoke, spoken* and *swim, swam, swum* must seem like our "to be" verb. For us, it's easy. For them, it's hard.

Hard though it may be, it gives our language more verbal texture. As a writer, that's critical to you. Naturally, our forebears were writers as well. Once they saw—as did speakers—that *-ing* was whipping weak verbs into shape, they figured: "Why not try this with strong verbs?" So they did, in the twelfth and thirteenth centuries. This was before Chaucer, who wrote in the late fourteenth century. By now English was changing rapidly. Vowels were shifting. People inside England couldn't understand one another. Something had to be done. Though *-ing* didn't solve the problem, it did open up verbs and make them more accessible, if you will. By the beginning of the fifteenth century this formation had taken such root that *-ing* was used with any kind of verb. It was at this time that Chaucer helped stabilize the language.

It wasn't all due to one man, but his work was so popular that it was read aloud and it was read, if at all possible, in his dialect. That's the dialect of English which you now speak. You don't speak Cornish English or Northumbrian. You speak the language spoken by this man of the court of Richard II and later of Henry IV.

Not only was *-ing* spoken by this time, it was written down. It was here to stay.

Perhaps *-ing* sounds pleasing to the English speaker's ear. Whatever the reason, it soon acquired all the functions belonging to a verb. For instance, it can perform genitive functions; it can possess. "Reading for reading's sake." Think of what that gives you.

It can be a plural. Comings and goings, feelings, drawings.

You can stick an article in front of it: a beginning. You can even give it an adjective: a good beginning.

If it can possess, can it be possessed? Yes. How about: Mary's savings grow?

You can enter a compound noun with it as either the first or the second part: shocking-pink or sightseeing.

You can also use -*ing* anywhere in a sentence, in any position occupied by an ordinary noun. Subject, predicate, nominative, and objective. Here's two for the price of one: Complimenting is lying. As an object, try: I hate lying.

You can govern -*ing* by an adjective: worth knowing. And you can govern it by a preposition: before answering.

Is -*ing* too much of a good thing? It's too late to know. This little device, so limited at first, has covered our language like ivy on a university wall. You can't imagine the school without it. Chaucer would be astonished, but being the practical man he was, he would lose no time slamming it on the page. No doubt, you're doing the same thing. I just did.

# DIALOGUE:
## THE SECRETS
## OF
## IDIOSYNCRATIC SPEECH

People are funny. No doubt you've noticed that others are not nearly as reasonable as yourself. Shocking, isn't it? This difference between you and other people comes out in speech. Obviously, difference displays itself in the subject matter people speak about, but on a deeper, more subtle level, it displays itself in the way in which they frame those very ideas.

Few writers write good dialogue. The main characters speak like their creator. That's tedious and homogenized. The plot may be terrific and the psychological motivation quite accurate. You're still riding on narrative, not on dialogue. Entire novels have been written with precious little dialogue. However, most novels need verbal exchanges between people. Also, why pass on heavy ammunition? Crackling dialogue is a joy to read.

Here's an example of what dialogue can do for you, quickly and efficiently. Two teenaged boys raise a racket. The noise disturbs their widowed great-aunt, a woman in her eighties. She says, "Please desist from your tawdry ravings." The boys quiet down. Wouldn't you? What's in that sentence? It tells you the old woman commands the English language. She understands precision and authority. If her niece, the mother of the boys, had yelled, "Shut up," it wouldn't be as effective. Everyone has heard "shut up." How

often have you heard "Please desist from your tawdry ravings"?
The novelty of the sentence grabs your attention. It also establishes
the speaker: She's well educated and most probably upper-class or
possibly upper-middle-class.

Speech is a literary biopsy. Suppose upon viewing white
people getting out of a flashy Cadillac or, worse, an Excalibur, our
widowed great-aunt wryly comments, "One gets the feeling they are
not Episcopalians." Again, one swift shaft of dialogue tells you
she has a keen sense of ethnic background. Is she racially prejudiced? We don't know that yet but we do know she does not enjoy
vulgar display of money. We also know, without her ever telling us,
that she knows who her people are and her place in society. She's a
WASP most definitely. She may be broad-minded, witty, and com-
passionate or she may be one of the blue-haired ladies who clings
to life with a parochial ferocity.

Upper-class people use more Latin-based words as well as
more subordinate clauses. They will cleanse sentences of obvious
emotion. The emotion is laid into the accuracy with which they
speak. Our great-aunt could have called the conspicuous consum-
ers "nouveaux riches assholes" but she didn't. Yet her sentence, if
thoughtfully considered, carries as much emotional information as
"nouveaux riches assholes." What upper-class characters choose to
tell you is as important as what they don't tell you.

This is not the case with lower-class characters: They'll usually tell you everything. They utilize more Anglo-Saxon root words
and their sentences are much simpler in construction than those of
middle-class or upper-class people. There is a glorious immediacy
to lower-class speech and if I boast, then cut me a break—this is
my class and my people and I love them. No turgid epiphanies clog
lower-class speech. No mildewed metaphors. Sock, bam, crash, you
get hit right between the eyes. There is also a marked tendency to
speak in Siberian absolutes. There aren't many shades of gray in
lower-class life; therefore, why expect hesitancies to be reflected in
speech? Speech always, always, always reflects a character's background and, more important, inner reality. Language is lived from

within. By the time you are five years old it is almost impossible to negotiate reality without language. Your brain talks to you in words; sometimes in pictures, sometimes in music, but most often in words.

What does this mean for your lower-class character? Here's an example: A welfare worker comes into the home of a poor woman. After the welfare worker leaves, the woman tells her son that the welfare lady came in "with the searching eye." Or my mother and her sister are in yet another fight (never an altercation). Mother refuses to give her sister a sweater. My aunt tells her friends that Mom is so mean she'd "skin a maggot." Mom replies that Wheezie is "black as the insides of a goat." Granted these are Southern expressions but they are poor-Southern expressions. Now for those of you not fortunate enough to live south of the Mason-Dixon line, let me explain that "black as the insides of a goat" is not a racial slur. It's a comment on one's emotional state. Goats eat the most appalling mixture of grains, garbage, glue. They'll even take a crack at the tires on your car. So a terrible mess, a perfect boil of bile would have to be the insides of a goat. Language comes out of real events, places, people. We were poor and we lived close to the bone. Our speech reflects this. There are no mechanical metaphors in our speech. We don't talk about "blasting off" or about someone being a "space shot" or a "space cadet." If someone's mentally defective (by our standards), we'll say, "Someone shot the dots off his dice." Language reflects reality: There's a lot of gambling and violence going on down there among the submerged tenth as opposed to the Four Hundred. Our first example in this chapter was a great-aunt. She's a member of the Four Hundred. I started out this life as a member of the submerged tenth. Chances are you probably started out in the middle classes and I'll get to their speech in a minute.

Urban lower-class speech is different from rural lower-class speech, and Southern speech is dramatically different from northern. But lower-class speech is more colorful and more direct than the speech of the other two large class groups.

If you mix in ethnic background you've added another interesting factor. Yiddish, Italian, Irish, Hispanic, Asian-American—these groups fed the English language beautifully. Television still rides on Yiddish expressions.

What about black speech? It's allied to Southern speech. Much as some whites want to separate from their black counterparts, linguistically they can't if they're Southerners. We're mixed up worse than a dog's breakfast. However, black Americans have secret speech. In this way they can confound the white man or speak right in front of him to another black. What a rich vein black writers and Southern writers have to mine. But there's a little problem: prejudice. This is encountered by any lower-class artist, especially a writer. It comes back at you in bizarre ways that make it hard to fight. Middle-class people don't mind us poor folks getting an education. However, they want us to emerge thinking like them, talking like them, and looking like them. Now this is not true for every middle-class person out there but my experience has been that the unwillingness to accept our version of reality is rampant. It's upsetting, I guess, to read the truth about our lower-class lives.

However, it's acceptable if a middle-class boy plays tough. Damon Runyon wrote about "low life" in a way that allowed the middle classes to accept it. The French call this *nostalgie de la boue,* or nostalgia for the mud. There's nothing wrong with that. It's entertaining. *My Fair Lady,* derived from *Pygmalion,* is based on this emotion. You can view the lower classes as amusing and you never have to feel the hunger or smell the despair. I have no quarrel with amusing people or even with sanitizing reality, so long as there are people out there who are *not* sanitizing reality.

Charles Rowell edits a literary journal, *Callaloo.* Were it not for *Callaloo,* one wonders what kind of start people like Alice Walker, Toni Morrison, Ntozake Shange, and others would have gotten. Writers who happen to be black still have a hell of a time getting published in the likes of *The American Poetry Review* or *The New York Review of Books;* the list is dismally endless. When asked why, Mr. Rowell gives this answer: "It's not so much racism as cultural imperialism. When an editor is reading a manuscript he may not know the writer is black, but he may find the themes and techniques contradictory to his own culture and dismiss the work. It's really a matter of education."[1]

Dialogue is a technique. That imaginary editor sitting in New York City, horribly underpaid (publishing salaries are the pits), probably doesn't understand the dialogue any more than the theme. How can you expect a fresh-faced, very bright young woman from Sarah Lawrence to "get" the phrase "black as the insides of a goat"? You have to educate her. So if you, like me, come from a "disadvantaged class" (how's that for a bullshit word?) you have to place the explanation close to the phrase and hope the reader picks it up. For instance.

Mother: "Louise, you are black as the insides of a goat!"

Louise: "You got no call to say such a thing to me, Julia. I am steady as a rock."

That is hardly the best exchange, but you get the idea. Louise has let you know that her mental state was called into question. If the reader still doesn't get it, there's not much you can do unless you want to gut your vocabulary.

Class hostility, as well as racial hostility, is alive and well in America. If you stay true to your background, there are people who aren't going to read you, or if they do, they'll attack you. Goes with the territory. Get tough.

A little sidelight on "class" words: *identify*, as in "I can identify with that." That's a middle-class person talking. Where I come from, the word *identify* is used when you go down to the police station.

A number of good books have been written about the state of the language. I've included a few titles below but you should go to a good bookstore and peruse the shelf on language. Buy a few of

[1] *The Daily Progress* (July 13, 1986), p. D1.

these and read them. You'll thoroughly enjoy yourself and you
might tighten up your own speech, too.

The following titles are scholarly works which demand concentration, but are very valuable:

Albert C. Baugh, *A History of the English Language*, 2nd ed.
(New York: Appleton-Century-Crofts, 1957).

Roger Brown, *A First Language: The Early Stages* (Cambridge,
Massachusetts: Harvard University Press, 1973).

Ernst Cassirer, *Language and Myth* (New York: Dover Publi-
cations, 1946). This is the most accessible of his works, but at
some point you should tackle the rest of his philosophical
works, much of which is language-based.

Noam Chomsky, *Language and Responsibility* (New York: Pantheon
Books, 1977). Chomsky has created intense reactions to his work,
both pro and con. I'm not taking sides in this academic debate.
You should acquaint yourself with his thought.

Paul Fussell, Jr., *Poetic Meter and Poetic Form* (New York: Random
House, 1965). This book doesn't have much to do with dialogue,
but it should be read.

Wayne Harsh, *The Subjunctive in English*, (Tuscaloosa: University
of Alabama Press, 1968).

Otto Jespersen, *Growth and Structure of the English Language*,
9th ed. (New York: Doubleday & Company, 1938).

The following titles are popular books, very easy to read and
quite enjoyable:

Charles Berlitz, *Native Tongues* (New York: Grosset & Dunlap,
1982).

Robert Claiborne, *Our Marvelous Native Tongue: The Life and
Times of the English Language* (New York: Times Books,
1983).

J. L. Dillard, *Black English: Its History and Usage in the United
States* (New York: Random House, 1972).

Stuart Berg Flexner, *I Hear America Talking* (New York: Van Nostrand Reinhold, 1976).

Leonard Michaels and Christopher Ricks, eds., *The State of the Language* (Berkeley: University of California Press, 1980).

Edwin Newman, *Strictly Speaking* (New York: Warner Books, 1974).

Middle-class speech is the primary form of American communication because the middle classes comprise the great bulk of the American population. Even given refinements due to age, race, and regionalism, these speech patterns are remarkably alike. In other words, the middle classes, wherever they may be, have more in common with one another than a poor Polish-American from Chicago has with, say, me. Every genre novel you read is written for the middle classes and written in their speech rhythms.

I create few middle-class characters except when I write for television. My fiction sticks to the very rich and the poor, usually colliding with one another. That's what I grew up with; it's what I know best. By virtue of seeking out people different from myself I can write middle-class dialogue. I'm surrounded by the middle classes. If you are a middle-class person, what follows will be redundant. You don't need to know it because this is your class. Your dialogue should be easy. If you are from a wealthy background or a poor one, read on.

The way I fashion dialogue for the middle classes is, I'm careful not to put in offensive metaphors. The speech is bland. It has to be. The middle classes are hated by the poor and despised by the rich. That's what being caught in the middle is all about. Therefore you don't want to offend anyone. Speech is soothing. One talks around issues. All government talk is middle-class talk at its worst. A wonderful television documentary is middle-class talk at its best. Your characters will usually fall between those two extremes.

Thanks to a generation of people in therapy, middle-class speech is excellent for describing emotional states. But it's done in a funny way (funny to me, anyway). Laura received a decent college education. She's thirty. She's having a fight with her boyfriend, who is a lawyer. She says, "You make me uncomfortable when you speak for me." (That's her version of a fight.) He might reply, "I'm not speaking for you. You were slow to reply to Tom's question and I stepped in." She replies, "You do this to me a lot. I think you've got to get more in touch with your feelings about women. Maybe down deep, you don't think I'm as capable as you are." And it goes on from there. Notice how careful they are. To me, this caution is the hallmark of all middle-class activity, whether it's speech or marriage. This isn't to say that our hypothetical couple can't scream and fight but it might take them longer to reach that boiling point than a couple from a different background.

What makes these characters so thorny for any writer, despite class background, is that it takes you twice as long to get the point across. Whenever you've got characters circling around an issue, you've got to put more on the page. People talking about feelings, as opposed to feeling/showing the emotion and acting on it, are a hard sell.

There's a flip side to this and that's when the middle-class character acts out. They go too far. Because they are so careful or repressed, if you want to use one of those dreadful psychological words, when they blow they blow big. The flower generation of the sixties (now agnostics of the Revolution in the eighties) was just such a blowout. This is not to say their political concerns were irrelevant, but underneath the legitimate political fury there was the tiniest element of nice girls and boys being bad girls and boys.

If there's no external event to give young people from the middle classes the opportunity to cut a shine (poor-Southern expression) then wait for their middle-aged crises. Indeed, much of middle-class fiction focuses on this period.

One of the ways a middle-class character knows how to be "bad" is to be "dirty." So a character in a crisis might use insulting sexual metaphors. Lots of "fuck this" or "fuck that" and lots of describing nonsexual states in sexual terms—for example, one man to another about a business deal: "They're hot. Let's slip them the meat."

Dialogue reveals. Even when your character is concealing his or her true emotions, you can use the dialogue as a counterpoint to this. A character is putting on a good face. The reader knows it. The dialogue gives you irony and perhaps, in this situation, poignancy.

Drug talk has been around since after the War Between the States, because that's when drug addiction began to be a national problem. However, the problem has escalated into an epidemic and our language, especially of the young, reflects this.

Nowhere does the older writer fall apart more obviously than when writing dialogue for the young, even without "drug talk." Is it because the older writer is hopelessly dumb? Possibly. But more to the point, television creates a generational consciousness in order to sell products. Young people are now commercially exploited. They are sold products in a language both borrowed from them and shaping them. They are encouraged to differentiate from other generations (the other generations are always stupid, venal, and do not understand them), and they talk in code. In a way, this code serves the same function as secret talk does for blacks. If you want to create adolescent characters, then you've got to crack the code. What's so awful about it from a writer's point of view is that in five years that dialogue will be hopelessly dated. The young person, by virtue of economic survival, must fit into adult society. The speech patterns change rapidly. The next generation of commercial victims is now ready for their moment of rebellious glory.

Be wary when using teenaged characters. If you're off the mark, they'll know first. If you're on the mark, you'll be old news soon.

Here's a snatch of dialogue to tell you why it's such a bitch. Young man to second young man: "Far out. I mean, like the theory of dialectical materialism is really what it's all about." Dead as a doornail. You bet. If I'd written it in 1968 it would have been right on, brother.

There is a geography of intellect. The brain locates function.

Speaking is separate from and not connected to your center for writing. The work scientists have done with aphasics is important for writers. Aphasia occurs when language centers of the brain are damaged. (Asphasia isn't a disease; you can't catch it. It is usually the result of trauma to the head.) For instance, a person harmed this way might know what milk is but he can't retrieve the word for it. So he'll look at you and ask for "white water." The ways in which intelligent people try to reconstruct speech after damage is important for us to know. Depending on the location of the injury, speaking, writing, or reading can be affected. A person might be able to speak but not be able to read the sentence she has just spoken. Reading or hearing these attempts to reconstruct language helps you go back to the basics. Language must be connected to reality. The words *red hot* instead of *fire* tell you something about reality. The speaker is getting as close as s/he can to the object/ event without being able to find the correct word. Aphasics help you see the world in a new way. They are speaking in English, yet it's a slightly different language.

I don't know enough about aphasics but in the ensuing years I hope to learn more.

Once when I was teaching a class on writing, a student who was a great fan of science fiction asked me how I would create dialogue for extraterrestrial intelligence. I replied that I wouldn't. I'll settle for terrestrial intelligence.

# CHARACTER DEVELOPMENT: BEING A THIEF OF SOULS

All human encounters embrace a magical quality. One strives to entertain, listen, learn and wink at frailty. Even if you never see that individual again she has left an invisible fingerprint on your soul and you upon hers.

Perhaps some of you have been accustomed to looking at the world through the prism of money and power. There's nothing wrong with that; our culture encourages narrowing our focus to external realities. People and Nature have the power to widen that focus. Emotion and spirit can become stronger realities than money and power. Most Americans get a whiff of this when they fall violently, romantically in love. This hit of suprarational life is a high. It's not irrational—it's beyond rational, and there's a big difference which I will explain more fully in the chapter on sub-junctive tense.

Falling in love has been a central theme of literature in Western culture. Romantic love enlivens characters sterilized by rationality. It's a potent form of magical encounter. But I repeat, all encounters possess a magical quality. As a writer you want your characters to reach your reader with their magic. The encounter should be as real as, perhaps even more intense than, if the character were met in the flesh.

Creating characters is enormous fun. Noncreative people think that writers make up characters and then jerk them through the plot. They talk about us playing God. It's not like that. If anything, the character winds up controlling the writer. For genre fiction—e.g., mystery, science fiction, Gothic romance—this is not true. Those are the suburbs of literature wherein the reader is invited into what is basically a verbal puzzle; it is always solved in the final chapter. That's fine and it's necessary escapism. Everyone needs it sometimes. However, the plot is the book. That's the definition of genre fiction. True fiction takes the writer places s/he has never been and calls forth deep emotions. The people are vividly real. Marianne Moore used to say that poetry was "imaginary gardens with real toads in them." It's true for the fiction writer as well.

Characters surround you. You will observe people much as an actor observes them. Every gesture, inflection, nuance is vital to you. You've got to pierce the exterior of people and bore into the center. You can't go about grilling strangers. You can do it to your friends but you might not keep them long. You'll have to learn to develop your powers of observation. You must become a thief of souls. Once you've "got" someone, you try to put her/him on the page.

You will rarely take one person, whole, and transfer him to fiction. Characters are almost always composites plus a touch of imagination. You distill people much as a liquor manufacturer distills grain.

Let me give you two examples.

*Example 1:* Tinker Lundstrom suffered in the hot vise of summer. He walked down Main Street wiping his brow with a red bandanna. Behind him an ancient Volvo backfired. Tinker hit the pavement and began crawling for cover.

*Example 2:* Tinker Lundstrom suffered in the hot vise of summer. He hated the heat. It reminded him of Viet Nam and those stinking rice paddies. Here he was, safe in Charlottesville, but he couldn't shake the fears that plagued him. He was okay until he heard any kind of loud report. He'd jump or hide and then, embarrassed, heart racing, he'd realize he wasn't in real danger.

There's nothing hideously wrong with Example 2, but Example 1 gets you into the character more quickly. The reader has been jolted by Tinker's response to a Volvo belch, just as Tinker was jolted by the event itself. As the story unfolds, you can reveal Tinker's fears and dreams. Example 2 in a flat, direct way, tells you about Tinker. You're a writer. You don't tell. You show. Example 1 shows you a character. Example 2 tells you about him. Example 1 is a distillation; Example 2 is still bran mash.

The most common mistake made by beginning writers in developing character is that they tell you too much. In fact, most of them give the background of each character as they introduce that person. The drive of the story gets stalled every time a new person walks onto the page. Dull. There's an easy way to avoid this sin. Before you ever start your novel, sit down and write out your main characters' histories. Then draw up genealogical charts so you can see, instantly as you work, who is related to whom. You'll see when characters were born and when they died. A short biography of your characters and their personality traits will also help you combine characters. A beginner's mistake in fiction is in fragmenting emotions into separate characters.

Real people have dominant traits allied with secondary traits. So do real characters. People can be contradictory and irrational. So can real characters; just be careful on the contradictions. If you do it too much it looks as if you are desperately manipulating your plot. If you have a character, however, who constantly contradicts himself, that can be funny. There, too, be careful. A character may serve the plot—indeed, s/he must—but if it is obvious, then your work will get suspiciously close to genre books, where the plot is the book and the characters merely devices. These books—e.g., Agatha Christie's mysteries—are fun to read but they aren't true novels.

The more you write, the more spontaneous you will become. Spontaneity is based on the knowledge we have acquired. When your characters become spontaneous—by which I mean they have a life of their own and they surprise you or even fool you—then you're doing something right. You are no longer pulling your characters through the novel. They are knocking you around at the typewriter. Don't be surprised if they wake you up at night either. This is a common occurrence, but many fiction writers won't talk about it. Our left-brain culture, top-heavy with facts and desperately low on imagination, takes such admissions as a confession of lunacy. How sad. We're losing our ability to see in Technicolor.

A black-and-white world is a nonfiction world. I read nonfiction constantly and I write it when there is no alternative. No matter how glorious nonfiction is, to me it always smacks of the term paper. Here's an easy way to see the difference between nonfiction writers and fiction writers, between left-brain people and right-brain people: They can run. We can dance.

Everyone has the capacity to use both hemispheres of the brain but America seems quite frightened of the imaginative hemisphere (Dionysius versus Apollo again) unless sanitized. All I can tell you is, if you hear your characters, if one of them shakes you out of bed at 4:30 A.M., protect that experience with your life. And thank the Muses because you're alive!

I went off on a tangent. Let me get back to character preparation.

Character biographies and genealogies help you keep things straight and they also help you define family characteristics if that's useful to your novel. Most family members, over generations, share common traits. Different though blood relations are on the surface, underneath they are surprisingly bound together. If you wanted to be nasty you could say the family is the transmission belt of pathology. If you want to be optimistic you could say the family is the cradle of love. For instance, although adopted, I, like a duckling, was imprinted by my adoptive parents and their family. We share one vivid family trait. We all have a sharp, biting sense of humor.

There's a family here in Charlottesville that's famous for their ability to breed. No matter what generation, they throw children like litters. Such details are not central to your character but they are informative. That's why you'll save yourself a lot of trouble if you map out your characters first.

Character is destiny. You've heard it before. It's true. The resolution of any plot must come from within the character. The redemption or destruction of any character is not the result of an external event (deus ex machina) but the result of that character's motivation. The inner life of people drives and manipulates their outer lives. If you remember that, the strange events that befall your characters will no longer seem strange. Wouldn't hurt to look at your own life either. We are the architects of our own Fate.

Granted, terrible things happen over which no one has control. You've got a character, young, female, enduring the siege of Richmond. Women couldn't vote. So the horror of war is visited upon her through no political fault of her own. However, what happens to her (short of a cannonball dropping on her head) within the framework of that war is up to her.

A compass need not see north in order to feel its pull. Ideas affect people even if they are not intellectual people. Emotions, even more than ideas, pull on people like that magnetic North Pole. Consider, again, our young damsel quivering on the anvil of war. She could have left the South before this mess. She didn't. That tells you she was either unconcerned with politics or that she loved her geographical place on this earth and was willing to brave the future. The excitement around her must have rubbed off. Bad though it was, it was never boring. The young respond strongly to that. We could further explore why this woman is in Richmond, but you get the idea. Her determination is the result of things she knows and things she doesn't, that hidden pull from the magnetic North Pole.

To explain the inner life of characters, at length, is to cheat readers of their own intelligence and experience. Show them people as they would meet them if the reader were in the book. Or let them imagine what would happen to them (without ever saying it directly) if the character stepped out of the book into the reader's real life. Let your readers figure out the character. Don't do it for them. Never insult your readers' intelligence nor take away the joy of discovery.

Within the context of character you will find the answer to the first basic problem of writing a novel. Do I write in the first person or the third? If you're quiet your main character will tell you what to do. First novels are traditionally written in the first person. Everyone gets that one for free. After that, the choice is difficult.

To write in the first person creates an immediacy, a closeness to that character—provided the character is, on some level, likable or fascinating. The trouble is, you lose a wide perspective. You can't give that perspective to your first-person narrator. If you did, she or he would have the mind of a god. She'd know too much, see too much. *Memoirs of Hadrian* by Marguerite Yourcenar is the only first-person novel I can think of whose narrator, of vast intellect, will not offend the reader.

By using third person you gain perspective, deeper irony, and a balance of emotions. You lose immediacy and you lose, to some extent, reader identification with your main character. Obviously, Margaret Mitchell solved that problem with Scarlett. Everyone identifies with Scarlett. However, such a strong connection to a single character using third person is difficult.

Again, your characters will tell you. Trust the characters. Don't manipulate them. It doesn't work.

Here's a first person voice:

"I attribute my success to Jesus. Since Jesus suffered for all of us I saw no reason for me to do it. Why be redundant? And more, how could I possibly be better than Christ? I firmly resolved to take a new tack and leave his record unchallenged. Let others look for their reward in heaven. I would seek mine here on earth. Of course, I had no idea it was going to take me so long."

What do you know about this person? You know the speaker is a Christian and probably a well-versed one, at that. Given the cadence of the monologue, it's a safe bet the speaker comes from the South. Where s/he lives now is unknown to you. You know this person is irreverent and has a fairly original sense of humor. You probably like the speaker unless you are some kind of religious nut. You don't know the speaker's age although the lighthearted irony probably rules out an adolescent.

Is this my inner voice? You'll never know. You don't even know the sex of the speaker. Here's an interesting aside. On the great issues of life—religion, death, purpose, community, war, peace, regeneration, and spiritual rebirth—the inner voice is androgynous. Virginia Woolf was right. We betray sex through relationships. Then we begin to sound like acculturated men and women.

Of course, there are people out there whose very being depends upon a mystical sense of sexual identification. So they would argue, passionately, that the above sentence is wrong and that every issue is colored by sex. It's a good argument and one that's fun. I've stated my position. I think once you've observed who is male and who is female, there is nothing more to say on the subject. Why belabor the obvious? I figure your hormones will take care of you. If you are a female, and a heterosexual man walks into the room, you know.

You can see from the first-person example how that voice reaches up and tugs at your sleeve. Go back to Tinker Lundstrom, our Viet Nam veteran. He doesn't tug at your sleeve but you're interested in him (I hope). Feel the difference?

When I teach writing I give out a set of questions that help students understand character. They have a month to complete the assignment if it's a semester course. On those occasions when I've filled in for a week, we do this in abbreviated form.

You must find people in the following age groups: twenty to thirty, thirty to forty, forty to fifty, fifty to sixty, sixty to seventy, seventy plus. They must represent a mixture of sex, race, and class background. Your assignment is to go out and interview them, asking the following questions:

1. What person or persons had the greatest influence on your life? Why?
2. How did you find the person you married, if you married? What

was it that drew you together? What kept you together or, if divorced, tore you apart?

3. When do you remember paying for things? Do you remember what a loaf of bread, a pound of butter, and a quart of milk cost when you were a child? What do you think about prices today?

4. Have you ever believed in an elected official? Why or why not? Are you politically active today?

5. What events outside your personal life stand out in your mind? (For instance, Mother remembered the news of the sinking of the *Titanic* and how the casualty lists were incomplete for days. She also remembered the *Hindenberg*.) These memories constitute what I call "generational birthmarks." My generation was shocked at the murder of John Kennedy. My mother was not. She'd seen assassinations before. Generations use events that assaulted them or uplifted them. They refer to them and are upset when a different generation does not understand the importance of the event. For instance, an older American who is black can tell you where she was when Joe Louis won the title. A younger black American might not care about Joe Louis but he might remember Muhammad Ali refusing to go to Viet Nam. Songs, books, films are also generationally marked. See if you can get your people to recall cultural events too. For some reason, people recall disasters first.

6. Where have you lived in your life? What place did you like the best?

7. If you had children, how did they change your life?

8. Can you recall expressions you used as a young person that you don't use today, such as "bee's knees," "far out," "swell"?

9. If you could tell other people something and hope they would remember it, what would you tell them?

On the appointed day the class would come in with their answers. It usually took a week to go through the material. Some students even brought in photos and tape recordings so we could hear the cadence of the people's speech. This exercise was the most popular of the chores I assigned. It forced students to develop interview skills. It got them out of themselves. Beginning fiction writers are often self-indulgent and self-obsessed. It taught them that other people know a great deal. Ultimately, I hope it taught them respect for people different from themselves.

After this material is digested, each student has to write a short story, in dialogue, between two of the people he interviewed.

The human animal varies from class to class, culture to culture. In one way we are consistent: We are irrational. Whenever you create a character you must allow for the existence of irrationality. I'm not saying that your characters beat their breasts before heaven because they're out of cigarettes. I'm saying: Use this fundamental of the human mind to enlarge your characters. Do you remember the scene in Tolstoy's *Resurrection* in which the judge, possibly bored, watches the defendant come into the courtroom? He decides to count the steps the accused takes and to base his decision upon whether it takes him an odd or an even number of steps to reach his seat. That's irrational and very funny.

Sometimes this is displayed by the author. In *War and Peace* there is a passage in which Tolstoy compares Napoleon to a little boy in a carriage who has been given "baby reins." The child slaps the reins around, yanks them, and thinks he is driving the carriage. Napoleon was like that child. The forces of history, not the child, hurtled the carriage forward. It's a lovely passage but highly subjective. Napoleon laid waste a great deal of Russia, burned Moscow, killed thousands and thousands of people. (Tolstoy's grandfather was in the war.) Although the Russians eventually won, it was at great price and not necessarily because of brilliant leadership. The weather proved a very effective general. Tolstoy so hates Napoleon that he can't give him credit for his contributions to history, to law, to government. So he mocks him in a vivid passage. That's irrational.

Some writers are especially attracted to deeply irrational states of being. Think of *Notes from the Underground* or *Crime and*

*Punishment.* If you want an American author, think of Truman Capote's nonfiction.

Most of us stay within the norm of human behavior. Murder is within the norm if one is threatened enough. Mass murder is not. Almost any extreme state provoked in a human will be accepted by the reader if the causes of that extreme state are carefully stated or shown. It's much more difficult to create sympathy for psychotic or totally evil characters.

Define *normal.* Maybe normal is the average of the deviance.

Finally I'd like to consider character types. There are definite human types recognizable in most cultures. There's the busybody and gossip. There's the humorless drudge. There's the constant worrier. There's the feckless partier. There are people who need enemies to give them identity. There are people ever spinning through the turnstiles of nostalgia.

You can't reduce human behavior to a simple set of responses, but you can recognize common strategies for facing life. You could have a very complicated character who bitches. That's how he handles stress. Your reader has seen that. It's familiar. Use the familiar to draw the reader deeper into the character, into what's behind the bitching.

Think of the zodiac. In a way, the zodiac has identified the twelve basic personality types for you. Each type has a good side and a bad side. The types are arranged on a wheel, which means no one type has precedence over any other type. Each person is then a combination of the good and the bad within his or her type. Whether you choose to believe in astrology is up to you. I always read my horoscope in the paper. It gives me something to believe in between breakfast and brushing my teeth at night.

If you wish the reassurance of twentieth-century research and conventional language, take the Myers-Briggs Type Indicator test. A trained management consultant or therapist can give you the test, which is a lark because there is no right or wrong answer, only your answer. Not only do you learn about your type, you learn about the other types in the two-hour interpretation. (I took the test in

October 1986, and it cost $100. I'm an INTJ, for those of you familiar with the terminology—but on a secondary level I've got lots of "feeling.") Personality is divided into sixteen personality types. These types are a shorthand course in character for a writer. However, don't get carried away with this. Use it as a guide. Your characters still must come from inside, must be felt. A character is more received than conceived.

*Please Understand Me: Character and Temperament Types,* by David Keirsey and Marilyn Bates, is a popular introduction to type.[1]

Write this on a piece of paper and stick it on your bathroom mirror: "Survival alters ideology." As life buffets you and your characters, this sentence will intensify in meaning. Change, growing from within and forced from without, is the mainspring of character development, of the process of human maturation.

---

[1] Distributed by Prometheus Nemesis Book Company, P.O. Box 2748, Del Mar, California 92014.

# PLOT,
## AS IN
# "THE PLOT THICKENS"

———————————— ■ ————————————

Most writers' manuals pay special attention to plot. Plots are broken down by category and sometimes you are given rules to follow which will help you construct a better plot.

It's probably a good idea to read those manuals and file away the information in the back of your brain. You need to know about people far more than you need to know about mechanical plot devices. Plot comes from character.

I believe there are four main plots. They are as follows:

The Self vs. The Self          Internal Conflict
The Self vs. Another          External Conflict (Personal)
The Self vs. The State        External Conflict (Impersonal)
The Self vs. Time/Nature     Perspective Conflict

For 99 percent of all novels, conflict is the core of the plot. Without it there is no tension and there's no reason to turn the page. Essays are the place for gentle reflection. Novels are not.

The fundamental conflict of life is The Self versus The Self. *Hamlet* best exemplifies this story line.

The Self versus Another is ably represented by Victor Hugo's *Les Miserables*. Although the pursuing figure represents the existing political order, the conflict is personal.

The Self versus The State can be viewed in two ways. George

Orwell's *1984*, wherein the State is the hero's country, or *War and Peace*, wherein the State is a foreign power, in this instance France.

A novel, a very great one, can embody all these conflicts.

I almost forgot an example for the fourth conflict. Hemingway's *The Old Man and the Sea*. The enemy is time. Time may not seem a suitable subject for a plot until you remember that death is the indispensable tribute that we owe to Nature. Time eventually brings death; and time, as much as an isolated act perpetrated by an individual, will change a character.

Every generation addresses these conflicts uniquely. Different cultures approach them uniquely. Can you imagine an American writing *The Stranger*? Can you imagine a Frenchman writing *The Adventures of Huckleberry Finn*?

Sometimes novelists get carried away and think they're writing philosophy. Philosophy is the knitting together of abstract nouns. Fiction is about emotions, not ideas. Ideas may be expressed in fiction and should be. But the heart of fiction, the pulse, is emotional. That's why you don't want to analyze the conflicts; you want to feel them. Your plot then involves an emotional resolution to one or more of the four basic conflicts.

There are three choices in selecting one of the plot skeletons. You can be comic, you can be tragic, or, thanks to Euripides, you can be tragicomic. Comedy takes more skill than tragedy. I used to think that tragedy was egotism, and comedy, realism. I no longer think that, but for a good decade that guided me in my choice of tactics. The reason I originally was disinclined to praise tragedy is that classical tragedy is about one human (a king or queen) pitted against the gods, whereas comedy could be about a human of any status enmired on earth with other humans. You cannot write a comedy without an acute sense of social relations and political power. (The politics can be implied, as opposed to expressed.) Aristophanes pitted humans against the gods in some of his comedies, *The Birds* being the outstanding example. Yet the floor of his plots was still relationships between people, between classes, between sexes. Sophocles didn't need to juggle that many players and subplots. Think of *Antigone*. (My favorite play of Sophocles is *Philoctetes*, produced in 409 B.C., not that anyone asked.)

Euripides saved us when he invented tragicomedy. This isn't to say that classical tragedies were not written after Euripides. *Macbeth* and *King Lear* fit the category. So does *Hamlet*, but I believe this may be the most overrated play in the universe.

I still prefer comedy or tragicomedy to classical tragedy, but the years have taught me that tragedy is not egotism but rather a necessary howl in the face of unfeeling Fate. We, the human race, need to raise our puny fists at the absurd cruelty of life, if only to remind one another we are not alone in our pain or in our perceptions.

I think the reason I choose the comic approach so often is because it's harder, therefore affording me the opportunity to show off. Also, a comic vision is my natural world view, but I've grown up in spite of myself and I can pass up the comic twist if it detracts from what my characters need. Yes, the life of a saint is hard.

"Comedy is tragedy plus time," Carol Burnett once said, and it's a marvelous insight into the creative process. Look at your plot shorn of the laughter, the irony, the broadsides. Chances are it could just as easily be prófoundly sad.

I have changed my definition of tragedy. I now think that tragedy is not foul deeds done to a person (usually noble in some manner) but rather that tragedy is irresolvable conflict. Both sides/ ideas are right.

Plot involves fragmentary reality, and it might involve composite reality. Fragmentary reality is the view of the individual. Composite reality is the community or state view. Fragmentary reality is always set against composite reality. Virginia Woolf did this by creating fragmentary monologues and for a while this was all the rage in literature. She was a genius. In the hands of the merely talented it came off like gibberish. You can use fragmentary reality without paying close attention to the community but the community/ composite reality is lurking somewhere beneath the surface. Think of *The Metamorphosis* by Kafka. In Stendhal's *The Red and the Black* the state is more obvious than in *The Metamorphosis* but not as obvious as in Gore Vidal's *Burr* or *Lincoln*.

Don't worry about balancing the view of the individual against the view of the community. The interface between the two realities will come out of your characters.

Are there more than two realities? I don't know, but I figure an open-faced sandwich is already metaphysical. Would God, as in the Judeo-Christian God, be a composite reality? No. If you wrote about God as did Milton, it would have to be as another character. The conflict would be The Self versus Another; in this case, the other is God.

The Greek gods present an interesting tableau. If you use the twelve Olympians, you have a composite reality because they are a definable community. They also represent a political order and fulfill the function of The State.

A sidelight about plot: chance. Chance is not the negation of certainty but an active force in human affairs. It can be positive or negative. Chance is not irrational. The Romans called it Fortuna and it may well be fortunate. Every one of us has bumped into coincidence, a streak of good or bad luck, and sometimes we've even had premonitions which have helped us. Those are examples of chance. How can you write about life and not use this aspect of it? Just don't overuse it.

Plot is the content of your novel. Content without style is propaganda or adolescence. Style without content is decadence.

If you're setting your novel in a time different from your own, remember that emotional relationships are more important than facts. While it's wonderful to be exact about the number of horses in the 1902 Kentucky Derby, it won't do you much good if you don't know your characters. What would have happened if Shakespeare had to make his plots historically accurate? Or if after reading Ovid he despaired: "It's all been said and done before." Unfortunately, you and I live in a nonfiction age. Shakespeare's contemporaries were more accepting of imagination and stronger than we are if you measure strength by the ability to face deep emotion.

The other thing to remember while plotting away is that people, like iron filings, will line up toward the center of force. For instance, if your setting is a small southern town and the sheriff is the real power in the town, then the majority of residents will support the sheriff. Many of them may not be conscious of this. To their way of thinking, this power is a given, therefore not examined. It's the way things are. On a national scale, you could say that the power rests with multinational corporations. Now it's hard to use corporate politics as an active force in most novels, but the fact that none or few of your characters ever question corporate power is a statement. Without realizing it, the characters have accepted the existing economic/political order as natural. In other words, they have lined up toward the center of force. Where is the external power in your story? I hope the internal power is with your main character.

Also, if you are using a community, a larger consciousness, think of buildings and corporations and professions (e.g., medicine) not just as accumulated capital or accumulated technical knowledge but as the sum of all prior human energies expended in their behalf. They represent permanent things with transient parts. Inanimate objects can exert a force over human beings.

Odd notes from my teaching curricula include the following:

> Morals are private.
> Decency is public.
> Novelty is not necessarily a virtue.
> Confession is not necessarily communication.

That's my shorthand to myself and I pass it along without elaboration. Perhaps those statements will be provocative and useful to you.

Here's a plot exercise for you: Write a short story about two gay waiters at the Last Supper. Smack my face! Maybe. Maybe not. If you are committed to literature you can't play safe. This plot exercise is one way to remind you of that in a somewhat humorous fashion.

The rule of thumb I've used for myself is that the more disturbing the plot, the more traditional the style. This may not apply to you but I want to ground the reader. I want to give her/him something to hang on to if the theme of the novel is on the cutting edge. (How's that for an overused phrase these days?) If the theme is not as disturbing, then I would take more chances with style. I have a novel I want to write someday about a woman's spiritual journey. This is a well-worn track, although in the past the redeemed have been men. I can take chances with style with this one. In *High Hearts* I examined a woman going into battle. Now women were going into battle disguised as men up until World War I, when physical exams became a rule. But the theme wasn't examined in literature, so it was a bit out there. Hence, I chose a conservative style.

You could be one of those people who can attack a difficult theme with a wild style. Virginia Woolf did it. Gertrude Stein practically invented the participle as style, but can you remember *what* she wrote about? Some writers find the exquisite style to match their subject matter. Turgenev, Alice Walker, and Charles Dickens spring immediately to mind.

For most of us, though, there's that San Andreas fault between what we're trying to say and how we say it. I pray for chance magnificence.

# THE SUBJUNCTIVE: THE EMPIRE OF THE SHADOW SENSES

If I were you, I'd read this chapter.

That sentence is in the subjunctive tense. English once had a breathing subjunctive tense. Over the centuries it has been strangled until it's gasping and so are we. We need this tense for full emotional and imaginative expression.

The *Oxford English Dictionary* defines *subjunctive* thus: "designating a mood the forms of which are employed to denote an action or a state as conceived (and not as a fact) and therefore used to express a wish, command, exhortation, or a contingent, hypothetical, or prospective event."

Using the *OED* definition, allow me to expand. The subjunctive tense is a state of being. Verbs express states of being as well as time. In Latin you know when you are placed in this new state of being because the language is inflected. I'll "inflect" an English verb. *Love* is present tense. *Loved* is past tense. Suppose you wanted to switch to the subjunctive tense. You'd say "lovedy." By stitching on a different ending—i.e., "y"—or, in some cases, by altering the inside of the verb (remember *drink drank drunk*) you let the reader or listener know he is on new terrain. That's inflection.

Just what is this terrain and why is it so important to you?

The subjunctive tense shines like an electric orchid. It's lush, exotic, and trembling. You enter the realm of the shadow senses: doubt; fear; illusion; magic; empathy so strong you can assume another being's identity; the future, undetermined as opposed to what we know as the simple future, or perhaps, put another way, dreams. The subjunctive allows you to do that without appearing crazy. You are invited to imagine, to participate, to wonder.

The English language in its current state discourages you from entering those realms. Your language demands that you state facts, prove them, and defend them. English is a language of hairline qualification. While that is useful, especially in a military and scientific frame of experience, it is not 100 percent useful for everyday life and it is dangerous for artists.

The English language can't keep you from feeling, fantasizing, dreaming, fearing, or stumbling into magic, but it can try to keep you from expressing what you have found while in those states of consciousness.

We have become so rigid in our experiential models that we label people irrational who dare discuss life in the shadow realm. I can't prove this and it's quite a leap but I have often thought that the burst of psychedelic drug use beginning in the late 1960's was an attempt to restore these valid experiences now denied us by our very language.

I would recommend a book to you which is technical but still very readable: *The Subjunctive in English,* by Wayne Harsh, published by the University of Alabama Press in 1968. I recommend this because it's filled with information but not combative. Linguistics tends to heated battles. As a writer you need to keep apace of linguistics while avoiding academic fights. (I'm tired of suffering expert knowledge. How about a little common sense?)

The subjunctive can't be restored to us by an Act of Grammar. We must approach the shadow realms by other paths.

*Shadow realm* has a ring to it, but so we're clear with one another, let me puzzle out what I mean. I believe that human experience can be lived on four planes: the arational, the irrational, the rational, and the suprarational.

An arational state of being is one in which human reason is irrelevant. I would classify plants and animals as arational. No, I'm not saying they can't think; they can. What I'm saying is that from a human perspective we can only gather information from these creatures and inanimate objects by observation. You can't talk to them. Well, you can but can they talk back? Language is a distinctly human quality. Therefore, arational life is life without language. Silence is arational. Life is much older than reason.

An irrational state of being is very human. It can be funny and it can be disastrous. Consider the following irrational thought process: "I will kill all my enemies; therefore everyone will love me." This has the compelling purity of logic although the premise is insane. The speaker doesn't realize the cause and effect of murder. Not only will s/he not be loved after removing those enemies, s/he'll be vilified, feared, or locked up. Irrational thinking can be expressed by language. It usually is, especially during our national political conventions. But then we trip over the irrational and border on the gross.

Rational thought is expressed by language. It might also be expressed by music and math, which are highly rational models of communication and related models, at that. This is where a speaker of English feels most secure and will try to twist other modes of experience into a rational model. We try to order reality within the governance of language.

The last state of being, and the one for which the subjunctive is most useful, is the suprarational. *Supra* is a Latin prefix that means over, above, or possibly, better. Suprarational does not deny logic. Irrationality denies logic. A suprarational state of being goes beyond logic but is based upon it. This is a silent state, since there is no vocabulary for it, but it is a silent state resonant with the remembrance of the word.

Maybe the following illustration will help. I've left out irratio-

nal, since it is in opposition to all three states of being. I've added
light to help you conceptualize.

| Arational | Rational | Suprarational |
|---|---|---|
| "Silence" | Talk | Silence (in English) |
| Animals/Plants | Language/Math | Comprehension |
| Inanimate Objects | Music | Apprehension |
| Infrared | The Spectrum | Ultraviolet |

Arational life predates rational life. (Think of the development
of an infant.) Suprarational life is dependent upon rational life. You
must go through rational states of being to get there.

The reason "Silence" is in quotes on the arational side of the
illustration is because there's sound in the animal world but it isn't
organized. Language is organized sound and agreed-upon meanings. The sound for *chair* means an object you sit in to any English
speaker anywhere in the world. Language is an exercise in
cooperation.

A classic exercise of Buddhism is designed to lead the initiate
away from language. "What is the sound of one hand clapping?"
Actually, I'd like to slap the monk across the face. That's the sound
of one hand clapping. But the point is to take people away from
words, to lead them toward "higher states of being."

An enduring stereotype of Anglo-Saxon culture is that the glib
individual is shallow. The strong, silent warrior is the ideal. Hell,
he's probably silent because he's stupid. Intelligent people usually
attempt to communicate.

The real anger toward the good speaker and writer comes
from envy of their power. Language is power. "In the beginning
was the Word." Why should a person be punished because she has
taken the time to learn language, just as the warrior took the time
to learn to fight? It's a skill.

I wonder if this distrust of expression isn't underneath our
gutting of the subjunctive tense in English. Were we getting too

close to the bone? If industrial life seeks to manage people's bodies, must it also manage their minds? Why would any culture, any language, seek to destroy a useful technique for the comprehension of and transmission of experience unless that experience challenged economic/political control?

Identifying with another human being is a basic experience. It's the heart of community. I say, "If I were you." That's about all I've got left of the subjunctive. *Was* is changed to *were.* Suppose I wanted to converse with the dead, another form of identification. (No, I don't mean call up spirits. I mean writing imaginary conversations, like Walter Savage Landor.) If I had the subjunctive to alert you, it might make the initial leap into this imaginative landscape easier for both of us.

If you and I had a healthy subjunctive, we could exchange certain ideas with ease. If we wanted to, we could discuss *déjà vu* without denial. We could portray a dream without shredding it via analysis. We could tiptoe into those border states whereby animals, plants, humans recognize their interdependency. We could listen to other people's musings and not force them to qualify their spirit. We would discover that the Latin word *anima,* meaning spirit or essence of a thing, animates the subjunctive. The subjunctive is about being, not about fact. It's about process, not about product.

Following are three excerpts which contain subjunctive verbs. I chose prose instead of poetry, since most of you are working in prose. Also, poetry was as highly specialized to the Romans as it is to us.

Since I'd rather be faithless to Latin and faithful to English, I asked a classics graduate student, Susan Johnston, at the University of Virginia, to translate these passages because I would take liberties with the translation.

The first section from Virgil's *Aeneid* is Dido's last speech before her death. She is filled with recrimination, regret, and a sense of betrayal. I cut lines 607–616, as there were no subjunctive verbs in those lines.

The subjunctive is underlined in the Latin and then again in the English translation.

The second and third translations are from Cicero. If you took high school Latin you remember the dear old chatterbox from your second year.

Cicero is fulminating against Catiline, a nobleman who attempted to overthrow the government in 63 B.C. The government at that time just happened to be headed by consul Cicero. Speaking to the Senate, Cicero relates the details of his investigation. Remember, this is political invective, and Cicero, a watershed figure in the development of his own language, is keenly aware of when he employs the subjunctive. For the record, Catiline fled Rome. His co-conspirators were caught and put to death at Cicero's insistence. Catiline was eventually killed in battle against government forces.

## VIRGIL, *AENEID IV*, 600–629

Non potui abreptum divellere corpus et undis spargere? Non socios, non ipsum absumere ferro Ascanium patriisque epulandum ponere mensis? Verum anceps pugnae fuerat fortuna.—*fuisset:* quem metui moritura? Faces in castra *tulissem implessem*que foros flammis natumque patremque cum genere *exstinxem,* memet super ipsa dedissem. Auxilium *imploret videatque* indigna suorum funera; nec, cum se sub leges pacis iniquae *tradiderit,* regno aut optata luce *fruatur,* sed *cadat* ante diem mediaque inhumantus harena. Haec precor, hanc vocem extremam cum sanguine fundo. Tum, vos, o Tyrii, stirpem at genus omne futurum exercete odiis, cinerique haec mittite nostro munera. Nullus amor populis nec foedera sunto. *Exoriare* aliquis nostris ex ossibus ultor qui face Dardanios ferroque *sequare* colonos, nunc, olim, quocumque dabunt se tempore vires. Litora litoribus contraria, fluctibus undas imprecor, arma armis: *pugnent* ipsique nepotesque.

Was I not able to tear apart his body after I had dragged it away and to scatter it on the waves? Was I not able to destroy his men with the sword or to place Ascanius himself on his father's table to be eaten? But the outcome of the struggle had been uncertain.—*It might have been*: whom did I, a woman about to die, fear? *I should have* carried torches into the camp and *filled* the gangways of the ships with flames and *killed* father and son with their kind and *thrown* my own self upon all those things … *let him beg* for help and *let him see* the undeserved deaths of his own men; nor, when *he has surrendered* himself to the laws of an unjust peace, *let him enjoy* his kingdom and the desired light of day, but *let him die* before his time unburied on the middle of the seashore. I pray for these things. I pour out these last words with my blood. Then you, Carthaginians, train your offspring and the entire future race in hatred, send these gifts to my ashes. Let there be neither love nor treaties between our peoples. *May* some avenger *rise up* from my bones *to pursue* the Trojan colonists with the torch and the sword, now, someday, whenever the power will present itself. Shores against shores, waves against waves, I pray, arms against arms: *let* the very descendants *battle*.

*        *        *

### CICERO, *IN CATILINAM*, I.6

Quid est enim, Catilina, quod te iam in hac urbe delectare *possit*? In qua nemo est extra istam coniurationem perditorum hominum, qui te non *metuat*, nemo, qui non *orderit*. Quae nota domesticae turpitudinis non inusta vitae tuae est? Quod privatarum rerum dedecus non haeret in fama? Quae libido ab oculis, quod facinus a manibus umquam tuis, quod flagitium a toto corpore afuit? Cui tu adulescentulo, quem corruptelarum inlecebris *inretisses*, non aut ad audaciam ferrum aut ad libidinem facem praetulisti? Quid vero? Nuper, cum morte superioris uxoris novis nuptiis domum *vacuefecisses*, nonne etiam alio incredibili scelere hoc scelus cumulasti? Quod ego praetermitto et facile patior sileri, ne in hac civitate tanti facinoris immanitas aut exstitisse aut non vindicata esse *videatur*.

For what is there, Catiline, which *can* please you now in this city?—in which there is no man outside that conspiracy of yours of ruined men who *does* not *fear* you, no one who *does* not *hate* you.

What mark of personal disgrace has not been branded on your life? What dishonor of private affairs does not adhere to your reputation? What libidinous desire has ever been absent from your hands, what crime from your whole body? To what youth whom *you had ensnared* with the enticements of corrupt practices have you not offered either a sword for boldness or a lighted path to desire? What indeed? Recently, after *you had cleared* a place for a new marriage at the death of your former wife, did you not also heap up another incredible crime upon this crime? But I omit this and I easily permit myself to be silent, in order that *it may* not *seem* that in this state the ferocity of such a great evil deed has either existed or has gone unpunished.

\*     \*     \*

## CICERO, *IN CATILINAM*, III.2

Atque ego ut vidi, quos maximo furore et scelere esse inflammatos sciebam, eos nobiscum esse et Romae remansisse, in eo omnes dies noctesque consumpsi, ut, quid *agerent,* quid *molirentur, sentirem* ac viderem, ut, quoniam auribus vestris propter incredibilem magnitudinem sceleris minorem fidem *faceret* oratio mea, rem ita *comprehenderem,* ut tum demum animis saluti vestrae *provideretis,* cum oculis maleficium ipsum *videretis.*

And I, when I saw that those whom I knew to be inflamed with very great madness and wickedness were with us and had remained in Rome, for this reason I spent every day and every night so that *I might realize* and *see* what *they were doing,* what *they were constructing,* and so that, since my speech *was* less convincing to your ears because of the incredible magnitude of the crime, *I might understand* this affair in such a way that as a result *you would* then at last *care about* your courage and your safety and *would see* with your own eyes the offense itself.

\*     \*     \*

Where did Virgil choose to use the subjunctive? "It might have been." This conveys a deep sense of longing not available to us in English. One word, *fuisset,* does this for Virgil. Look at the other underlined verbs. They are each about an event, an action that could easily have happened but did not happen because the speaker, Dido, decided against doing these things. But she's having second thoughts. She's torn apart by doubt, by her loss, by her own warring hatred and love for Aeneas. The English gives you the literal meaning of the verbs, yet the emotional shading is gone.

Cicero is even more clever. Right off the bat he attacks his enemy by asking what *"can* please you?" It's the subjunctive tense. There's so much hidden here. Cicero implies not just treason but that, emotionally, Catiline has ruined himself. Rome is the center of the world. Nothing in Rome *can* please Catiline. Therefore, emotionally, Catiline has cut himself off from Great Mother, Rome. He will never be happy.

Cicero then continues to build his case with a brilliant mix of regular verbs with the emotive subjunctive. If I were Catiline, I would have fled, too!

Are you beginning to sense what we have lost? I could write the following in the subjunctive and it would have a twist, a pinch of poignancy it does not have now: "It rained today in the Blue Ridge Mountains and the tears turned to violets." I could change *turned* to *turnedy* my made-up subjunctive device, adding a "y," and you would begin to hear my inner music. As the sentence now stands it has a slight poetic ring but I have to drag you along to get you to join me, mentally. With the addition of "y" for the subjunctive tense, you would be with me instantly.

Much of what we now regard as silly or crazy is not. Remember when people who saw auras were thought to be loony tunes? Kirlian photography was developed and now any person may see an aura. The aura was a true state of being. Some could see it. Some could not. Because fewer people could see it than not see it, it was deemed an unacceptable apprehension of reality. There are events, states of being, that are absolutely true, but today, they cannot be proven or rendered rational via Aristotelian logic. (Aristotelian logic rests on the paradigm which is a specific pattern. Think of it as a mental equation.) Here's an example:

> A: All birds sing.
> B: Madonna sings.
> Synthesis: Therefore, Madonna is a bird.

The paradigm is only as good as its original assumption. Much of what we assume must be questioned. I can forgive noncreative people swallowing everything whole. You are an artist. You can't be forgiven. You must question. It would be easier if you had the subjunctive to help you but you don't. You'll have to do the best you can inside a culture which is becoming increasingly unimaginative.

Despite the culture, an artist must live without fear of emotion, of other types of consciousness, of suprarational experiences. Whether Americans will loosen up, will embrace life, is anybody's guess. If they don't, you'll spend your life in deep rebellion against your own culture. Let others live in black-and-white; you must live in Technicolor. And without a subjunctive tense you must still make your reader see the blood at the heart of the ruby.

# A SIDELIGHT ON ENGLISH PREOCCUPATIONS

How many phrases or words can you come up with for death? Passed away, crossed over, bit the dust, bought the building (or farm), iced, checked out, gave up the ghost, pushing up daisies, met his Maker, kaput, done for, expired. Bet you can come up with more.

Now, give me phrases or words for love. Admiration, adoration, attachment, devotion, infatuation, passion, tenderness, yearning, cupid, inamorata, swain, sweetheart, care for, cherish, desire, dote upon, endear, fancy, lose one's heart, pay court, prize, revere, amorous, beloved, enamored. While there are many love terms none of them quite seems as powerful or as pure as the word love … but then none of the euphemisms for death are as powerful as the word death. If anything, these counter terms rob the event of its shattering power. Perhaps we are trying to slide away from love and death.

What does this tell you? How deeply engrained in our language is the fear of emotional life.

A Russian speaker can indicate to a listener the nature of his/her relationship with, say, Mary. By altering Mary to Marushka or Marushkaya or Marushinka, or whatever, he tells you if he is a friend, a family member, a lover, and so on. Please don't take my fiddling with Mary as legitimate Russian grammar. I once lived in the White Russian section of New York City and an old woman (already in her eighties in 1969) in my building used to talk to her cat, Marushka. This woman spoke very little English and I spoke no Russian. Over the space of two years we learned to communicate. After all, we both loved cats.

When I began to apply myself to Russian literature, erratically I confess, the old lady and her cat served me well. No longer could I be sidetracked by Natalie becoming Natasha or the other welter of Russian nicknames. Those nicknames serve a vital emotional/social function.

The closest we have is "honey" and that's about it unless you want to have fun and trot out the most ridiculous "pet names" you've ever heard.

But the point stands: English is weak in describing emotional states or intensities of interpersonal relationships.


P.S. If I ever get another kitty I think I'll call the feline Pusskin. No, I am not catless. I have five. Much as I would like six—more for the complete complement of Muses—five is enough!

# Myth and Symbol, as Opposed to Hit or Myth

After World War I the Western world began to disengage from its own past. This unhappy process was accelerated after World War II, which was, historically, Act Two of World War I. Was life before the Great Wars a momentous caesura or was it a Golden Age, within memory but forever out of reach? Perhaps if one were wealthy, the ninety-nine years from 1815 (Waterloo) to 1914 were as close as humans can come to frolicking in the Elysian Fields.

Fifty-five million people died during World War II, and that's a rough estimate. Add the forty-two to forty-five million casualties from World War I, and the murdered ghosts call to us as plaintively as Banquo at Macbeth's banquet.

Not only was the Western world shaken to its foundation but the Eastern world also lurched in a new direction. China became a communist nation; India, a free one; and Japan shocked everyone. Africa, neither East nor West, pursued her own destiny with no help from the West or the East, and, as with the rest of us, her pursuit involved killing. If ever there was a century drenched in blood it is our own.

Small wonder that the Western world wanted to forget its past, submerge its heritage and, like a foolish child, focus on the present.

People are like pieces of a puzzle. They have a past (ignored or expressed), a present, and a future. If we could figure out how to fit ourselves together we'd have the answers we need for peace, prosperity, and maybe, just maybe, happiness as a community. So here's my little piece of the puzzle in literary/cultural terms.

Casting aside three thousand years of cultural integrity is a form of intellectual mass suicide. Our literature begins at 1184 B.C. if you will take the fall of Troy as a beginning. Classical scholars can argue about the date, but in literary terms this date is fixed at 1184 B.C. Homer wrote about the war in the ninth century B.C., although, again, one can argue about dates. For a writer, for an artist, the exact moment is not as important as the sense of a beginning. This is where we begin.

Both concurrent with this beginning and predating it is the literature of the Jews. These two strains of cultural experience weave together some thousand years after Troy in the catacombs of Rome. Every Western writer—Russian, French, English, Czech, Hungarian, etc.—every single one of us everywhere on the globe rides bareback with a foot each on two mighty, conflicting horses: Greco-Roman culture and Hebrew-Christian culture. As Greece was mother to Rome, so Judaism was mother to Christianity, which in turn was mother to Islam. (However, Islam is not part of the Western world culturally, except through Spain.) How does one marry the clear, hard thinking of the Greeks to the mysticism of the Hebrews? How does one recognize the contributions of the Twelve Olympians when one is taught there is only one God and knowledge of any other God is the road to death? Saint Augustine struggled to bring together these two opposing cultural forces. He's worth reading for that reason alone. (When you read him you'll find many other reasons to relish this remarkable man.) You and I, in a variety of ways, will continue this struggle, although by now the balance has tipped way over to the Hebraic-Christian side of the cultural equation.

One of the reasons our culture has become lopsided is we've tossed out Latin as a requirement for college. Through Latin came the sense of our original heritage. We were Greeks/Romans before we were Christians. Latin taught us how to think, how to read critically, and how to learn our own history. We've jettisoned much of that history and with it three thousand years of shared, universal symbols.

The Olympians were universal even when they were no longer invested with the power of human faith. They retained the power of myth. Any writer of the Western world could use these myths for his/her own purposes. In a sense, it was cultural shorthand. For example, Byron could write, "Rome that Niobe of cities," and any literate person would know he was representing Rome as a city of repeated anguish, sorrow, and humiliation. Niobe's story was familiar to everyone.

Briefly, so you can realize the impact of Byron's imagery, here's the story of Niobe: Niobe was the daughter of Tantalus. (A bad character if ever there was one. He served his son's flesh to the gods. This was not appetizing to the Immortals so they sent him directly to Hell. He did not pass Go and he did not collect $200. In fact, he's probably still down there being "tantalized.") Niobe was a much better soul than her father but she did have one vice. She burst with pride over her fecundity. Seven sons and seven daughters she brought to life; fourteen healthy, beautiful, glorious children—perhaps Niobe can be forgiven her pride. However, she made the mistake of rubbing in her maternal achievements to Leto.

Now Leto was the daughter of Titans, which means she was older than the Olympians. The Titans came first and like the *Titanic,* their namesake, they sank. But that's another fabulous story. Leto had only two children, twins, conceived by Zeus. Zeus's wife, Hera, seethed with rage. Poor Leto crept into hiding when she gave birth to Apollo and Artemis. Zeus, usually a gentleman where ladies were concerned, brought his babies up on Olympus. Hera's idea of fun was not in being a stepmother but she survived.

Leto suffered enough, thanks to Hera's blasts. She never bore more children. Her son and daughter loved her. Niobe's taunt so enraged them that Apollo and Artemis put arrows to their bows and slew all fourteen children. Yes, it was excessive, but from

Apollo and Artemis's point of view, how dare a mortal (read: slug) insult an immortal, their mother? She must be made to pay for her insolence; otherwise more humans would get saucy.

Niobe, crushed, never regained her composure. She wept continually and turned into a column of stone on Mount Sipylus in Lydia. Water ran continually from the stone column.

If you knew mythology you'd know all this. With one word, one loaded proper noun, Byron could pull your heart out.

It's possible to reclaim what is ours, but only if we return Latin to the secondary-school curriculum. I don't mean as an elective; I mean as a requirement for collegial studies. We consign our children to ignorance and then wonder why they behave as they do. Not only can the young not understand history, they can't understand Christianity. Christianity grew on the soil where Niobe weeps, and its center, to this day, is Rome.

Let's take the worst scenario: Americans remain ignorant. They throw the baby out with the bath water, and only the faintest trace of mythology remains. Where does that leave you and me as writers?

You can continue to use mythology but it had better be one of the baby myths—by which I mean one that is known by everyone. For example, almost everyone visually knows Medusa. They may not know why she has snakes for hair or how she turned into such a viper (couldn't resist) but they know she is a symbol for evil and for turning mortals to stone. Think about turning to stone for a minute. Isn't it a sensational image for evil? One becomes immobilized by hate. Didn't Dante do this in *The Inferno*? Satan is encased in ice. Symbolically, Satan and Medusa are connected.

Okay, you can use an easy myth. You can use more "learned" ones only if you explain them as I have just explained Niobe.

What can you use? What symbols are shared? You can always use the Bible. Moses, Ruth, Mary Magdalen are vibrant symbols/people. The catch is that many of your readers may not be Christians and therefore not familiar with the Old and New Testaments. In America, Christians are the great majority but there's a healthy minority of people who are not Christians. And what about the Christians who don't read the Bible? Baptism was the extent of their religion. They scooted out of the church. Again, even if one is not religious, why cast aside nearly two thousand years of history, of symbol?

Given the violent fluctuations within Christianity itself, one can unwittingly arouse fanatical hostility by using Christian stories and symbols. It's worth the risk. Go ahead and use them.

One can descend from myth and symbol and utilize current shared images, such as those in advertising. This is restricted by nation. The ads of Germany are not the ads of America, but if you narrow your audience to only your nation, you can use this. The problem here is that advertising is trivial and short-lived. You'll gain quick applause and then your book will be dead as a doornail in five to seven years' time.

You can also use psychology for your metaphors but you're on trembling ground. First off, psychology is a set of beliefs shared by the affluent. Secondly, it does not represent human emotion/behavior but, rather, attempts to explain them quite literally. Thirdly, the originators of this system of thought robbed Greek mythology for nomenclature—e.g., Oedipus complex. If you wish your books to be understood only by middle-class people with limited references (the bulk of book buyers in the United States), you're fine. The poor don't go to therapists, any more than they go to lawyers. Then, too, psychology suffers fads just like fashion. Your brilliant delineation of a midlife crisis might be upturned by the next "in" form of self-understanding. If psychology were a science it would be easier to use, but it isn't. Experiments with rats do not necessarily apply to humans. We'd be better off if they took the humans that acted like rats and put them in a maze.

One might even agree that popularized psychology has hurt the American novel. What American man today would have the guts to write an honest novel about his relationship with his mother? They'll write far more about their fathers than their mothers, possibly for fear of being labeled Oe\    al. (Oedipus kills his father and marries his mother. He does not know his parents, so this is not as horrible as it might be.) If a man is going to write about his mother, he can play "safe" and make fun of her or in some way belittle her. By the same token how many novels can you recall written after World War II by a woman about her relationship with her father? (The female version of the alleged Oedipal complex is the Electra complex.)

The other danger about popularized psychology is, it tempts a writer to tell instead of show. Characters must never be explained. They must be *revealed*.

Look, I am not discussing an individual's need for therapy. I am discussing literature. If you substitute psychology for a developed belief system (mythology, Christianity, etc.) what you do is encourage gross narcissism. Psychology is about one person traveling through the labyrinth of his life to the dreaded Minotaur. If he can conquer/understand his Minotaur (if you don't know mythology, then substitute for *Minotaur* "the origins of his unhappiness"), he emerges victorious. How many such journeys are really interesting? Even if you can conquer your own monsters, what about the world around you? Psychology as metaphor is very limiting—and to my way of thinking it's hopelessly boring.

It's extremely difficult to use science for metaphor. Science is so ·fragmented and specialized that anything beyond high school science will lose your reader. People can write books about science and make it popular, but that's nonfiction. Fiction and nonfiction have nothing in common. You need shared symbols. Science will not give it to you except for a science event like walking on the moon. As to science fiction, that is a genre and therefore inhabits the suburbs of literature. Also much of the "science" is invented and therefore not a true symbol accepted over the centuries. In a way, it's close to advertising. To the best of my knowledge, only H. G. Wells and Jules Verne have transcended the category of science fiction.

What about astrology? Yes, it is a shared symbol but it's become so debased that you can't use it with pride. You can use it for comic intent. Keep in mind that astrology is really the remnants of pagan philosophical and astronomical knowledge and was attacked and continues to be attacked by fundamentalist Christians. It has withstood almost two thousand years of spite, but it is not a legitimate belief system for literary application. You could write some great mysteries based on it though.

Lastly, sex. Is this a universal symbol? No. Absolutely not. Sex is a biological function and an emotional joy (if you're lucky). It is not tied to the mysteries of the universe, it does not connect with intellectual belief systems—in fact, it is usually suppressed by them—and finally, it gets old fast. The joining of plumbing parts between the opposite sexes or the same sexes can't hold the weight that a developed belief system can. By "developed system" I mean a set of symbols, stories, characters that represent every human emotion, every human circumstance, and every human fear and hope. There must be retribution and redemption (even if only by chance) for a system to have power over the minds of humans. The Greek myths have that power. The stories of the Old and New Testaments have that power.

Sex does not enter into the compromise of history. Mythology and Christianity do. I'm not saying you can't use sex in your fiction. I'm saying you can't expect it to carry the load of shared meaning.

Assuming you know your Bible and need no instruction, let's turn to the Olympians, those twelve gods, each with jurisdiction over aspects of the universe and human life. They lived together on Mount Olympus in Greece. This mountain forms the boundary between Greece proper and Thessaly and overlooks the Vale of Tempe. (*Vale* as in big valley, make a great name for a TV show.) You can read about the gods somewhere else. I'm examining them for literary use. I do suggest Edith Hamilton's *Mythology* and her *The Greek Way* for beginners, as well as *God and Heroes* by Gustav Schwab, and H.D.F. Kitto's *The Greeks*. They will get you started.

The gods form the first family in literature. I define a family as a gathering of people related by blood (or adopted) with conflicting interests. Six women and six men, with extraordinary powers, squabbled with one another, loved one another, and dallied in human affairs for comic relief. The women had equal power with the men. One man ruled this brood because he had a bit more power than anyone else. This is Zeus. He also had a wandering eye and his offspring were often half-human, half-god. You might want to think of them as the first angels, for in a way, they were. Other offspring of the gods were half-human, half-beast, which is another sharp insight into human behavior. Nothing escaped the Greeks. They knew us better than we know ourselves. They weren't afraid. Modern man is not nearly as emotionally hardy as his ancestors.

What's so important about these twelve gods is their legacy. They left a body of symbol that is relevant to the human condition. They also left a form of worship in which there is no guilt. One might fear a god or goddess but one did not go down on one's knees. Kneeling was for slaves. You could talk with your god, man to Man, woman to Man, woman to Woman or man to Woman. You could also bribe them (at your peril). You, the human, had some dignity and even some power. You could hurt a god but usually you paid with your life. And you could write about them—endlessly. The Olympians were vain. They wanted humans to know about their deeds. The writer performs an important function for the gods.

The other interesting aspect of the gods is that they represent a recognition of left brain and right brain functions. To take it at its most watered down form: the left brain is the logical side, the right brain is the creative side; the left brain is analytical, the right brain is a synthesizer. (Read Julian Jayne's *The Origin of Consciousness in the Breakdown of the Bicameral Mind.*) As far as I know, no one has ever perceived the gods in this light but let me categorize them in this fashion.

| *Left Brain* | | *Right Brain* |
|---|---|---|
| Apollo | | Dionysius |
| Athena | | Aphrodite |
| Hades | | Poseidon |
| Hermes | — Zeus — | Artemis |
| Hephaestus | | Hera |

Zeus combines both functions. All these Olympians can behave irrationally but their primary functions and personality type, for me, fall into right brain or left brain. Once again the Greeks are ahead of us, or else I'm reading too much into their stories.

Think of the fun you could have using this information symbolically. Wouldn't Dionysius be the god that drove Janis Joplin over the brink? Wouldn't Apollo be the hidden force behind Buckminster Fuller, while Artemis was behind Martina Navratilova? Imagine a novel wherein the main character not only uses mythological symbol but interacts with that deity closest to his/her state. Just an idea.

If you never plan to use the gods, you still need to know them. As a writer you need contact with other prewar writers. Ignore mythology, and the force of writers before World War I will be lost upon you.

# WRITING AS A MORAL ACT

Language is decanted and shared. If only one person is left alive speaking a language—the case with some American Indian languages—the language is dead. Language takes two and their multiples.

Speaking is a social contract. You and I agree to exchange sounds whose organized noises represent agreed-upon symbols. *Cat* means the same thing to you as it does to me. It doesn't mean a thing to a Portuguese person. You might think of a sleek tiger cat and I might be thinking of a long-haired red cat but we are in sync about the species. If you want to get fancy you could say feline (Latin again) but we're in the same ballpark.

While talking about Miss Puss we assume that speech will follow a predictable order. An English speaker must have this assurance, since our language is not inflected. You do not have the liberty to scramble words. When native English speakers hear foreigners (there's a word worth researching) speak, they often laugh as the foreigners struggle with our word order. We complain about the tyranny of conjugation and irregular verbs in Latin. Complain as you will, Latin gives you a stylistic freedom not available to you with English. Our cat conversation proceeds along a well-worn track. However, you can spice up this locked-in word order with glittering adjectives, extraordinary vocabulary, plus your own special voice control. When you put this conversation on the page you lose the voice control, so you are ever more dependent upon your command of vocabulary, cadence, and your own imagination.

Up to this point we are in agreement. We are cooperating as two individuals conceding to civilization. Literacy, or even simple speech, is the starting point of civilization. The unspoken truth is that we are unequal; we are different. If you and I were exactly the same, a pair of identical strangers, we wouldn't need to speak to one another or to write. You'd know what I was thinking and vice versa. All communication rests upon inequality. That's the sheer excitement of it. I don't know what you think. I can't wait to find out. Language is the common thread by which we explore our differences and, if we are both lucky and mature, the thread that will bring us to a form of agreement or at least understanding.

Therefore it is imperative that people write and speak the truth. There can be no community if a person is not as good as her/his word. How easy to write that and how hard to put it in practice. You, my reader, whoever you are, know things that will disturb others. You must tell. Camus said, "It is immoral not to tell."

Again we can split hairs. A dear friend of mine has put on ten pounds. Do I say, "Gee, Frank, you're fat as a toad" (the truth) or "Frank, you look wonderful." It may be wonderful to see him but he still looks fat. I'll choose to make my friend feel better.

If Frank, involved in a sordid affair with the wife of another friend of mine, asks my opinion, I'll tell him the truth. "Either she leaves him and goes to you or you leave her. Don't mess with married people."

Telling the truth should be simple. Writing the truth should be even easier because you don't have to look your listener/reader in the eye. Writing the truth is far more treacherous. The act of putting words down on paper gives them a glamour and perma-nence not associated with speech. Writing, to most everyone, is a more serious act than speaking.

Every generation produces those people—writers, composers, plastic artists, and even the re-creative artists—who shatter social

convention and tell the truth. They aren't saying "Here I am."
They are saying "Here you are." The "you" is both individual and
plural. In the case of *Oedipus Rex* or *Crime and Punishment*, this
recognition can be horrifying. In the case of *The Birds* or *School
for Scandal* it can be deliciously funny.

If this is prevented from happening (as in Stalin's Soviet
Union, Hitler's Germany, Botha's South Africa) the civilization
begins to die from the inside out. There may be a plethora of books
in such nations but they aren't upsetting. They merely entertain.
Art must both entertain and provoke.

If people refrain from telling what they know, how long before
they actively lie? Is there not a subtle and corrosive connection
between withholding the truth and lying? You are as sick as you
are secret.

If you don't believe that words will be followed by deeds, how
can you trust anyone? How can you form a community? When
language no longer corresponds to reality, any form of betrayal and
misconduct are to be expected.

Writers are the moral purifiers of the culture. We may not be
pure ourselves but we must tell the truth, which is a purifying act.
Therefore it is impossible for a real fiction writer to be the
mouthpiece for a political cause. A writer should, as should any
citizen, cherish his or her political beliefs but that's not the same
as being a propagandist.

By political beliefs I am not talking about the American
two-party system. The Republican party is a study in unlimited
vandalism, and the Democratic party presides over the cadaver of
liberalism. The difference between Republicans and Democrats is
the difference between syphilis and gonorrhea. Political beliefs are
stronger than that. The separation of church and state is a political
belief. Affirming or repudiating capital punishment is a political
belief. The desire for a state-controlled economy is not only a
political belief, in some nations it's a religion. You get the difference. Our political parties skate over the political fashions that are
current. Opportunism wears many masks.

Since politicians seek to conceal the truth in order to dupe the public, every writer alive is critical of whatever political system s/he lives in. Not everyone in politics is bad and politics is a necessary evil, *but* politics is never ever about the truth. Politics seeks to conceal; Art, to reveal.

The severest blasts in Russia or in our own country are directed at people the state considers expendable. First, writers get it because they are potentially dangerous. Scientists run into walls only if they become critical of the uses of science by the government. If they shut up and continue as the hired help, they're okay. In our country we are too sophisticated to put writers in jail. It looks bad. Also, we are very fortunate in that most of our elected officials are semi-illiterate and therefore they don't even know what we're writing. Should a writer happen to become disturbing and powerful enough to come to the attention of our civic worthies, then the fur flies. A politician will cite the offending author and make a stink. His acolytes will press to have the subversive texts banned from the libraries. (Actually, the acolytes control the politician. S/he usually responds to their pressure.) Loathsome as it is, such talk does get into the newspapers, and once publicity attaches itself to a book, the sales shoot upward. Bless the narrow-minded! You can survive that. You'll know when you're really in dutch when the IRS hounds you. You think a highly placed government official wouldn't stoop that low? You think the IRS is not a punitive instrument of whatever administration is current? You also believe in the tooth fairy, don't you?

Communist and fascist nations recognize the power of writers. They imprison them or drive them out of their homeland. The United States of America, no matter how absurd and contradictory our various administrations, has drawn the line here. When push comes to shove, we defend the First Amendment. Today, in 1987, that Amendment is a political hot potato but I trust it will flourish intact. By defending the First Amendment we are defending writers. Buried in the marrow of our collective bones is the recognition that we must know the truth about ourselves. Even the most bigoted American hates a liar. Despite our economic struggle, far better to be a writer here than elsewhere.

Morality is involved in issues other than lying or withholding information. What happens when the word is substituted for the deed? Some act of faith is always involved in the connection between theory and action. To write and talk and not produce the action is to destroy faith. Once again, community becomes impossible.

The best example I can think of for this phenomenon involves the protest movements of the late 1960's and early 1970's. While the Nazis committed unspeakable acts (I mean unspeakable—they had no word for what they were doing) the New Left and the Women's Movement spoke incessantly but committed few acts. This seems to be a hallmark of leftist politics: the substitution of the word for the deed. Yes, some things got accomplished but compare it to the dedicated raising of money by the New Right and the intelligent daily application of those funds and you quickly grasp the difference.

The New Right has few writers. The New Left was top-heavy with them. From the New Left true fiction writers emerged, leaving behind the restrictions of ideology and moving toward a wider embrace of human experience but, I hope, imbued with a belief in justice, equality, and innovation. To date, not one decent fiction writer has emerged from the New Right.

I was one of those people to emerge from the New Left. I recall the early days of the movement. The blind were leading the blind with great excitement into walls, into ravines, into the waiting rifles at Jackson and Kent State. These anguished memories are then supplanted with pride; we did help to end a war which was ill-conceived. We wrested a few changes from the system for the nonwhite and we created the conditions for the removal of a President who may have committed criminal acts. From this haunted terrain sprang a generation of scribblers. Perhaps the New Right will fool me yet and bring forth fiction writers capable of making us see ourselves as we really are. One thing is certain: That writer or those writers will get clobbered by their former associates. The Right suffers little dissent.

Some writers maintain that they are apolitical. A worm is apolitical; a human being is not. If you live in a political system and do not seek to make it better you are still a product of that system. Your lack of involvement is a political statement. All Art rests on a political foundation but it need not concern itself with politics.

Go back to *The Iliad.* Achilles has plopped his butt in his tent and won't fight. Agamemnon took a damsel awarded to Achilles for his battle prowess. Briseis was her name and Achilles, although in love with Patroclus, a man, wanted the girl. Why not eat your cake and have it too? The Greeks were not as ravaged by sexual definitions as we are. Agamemnon, as head of the armed forces (think of him as Eisenhower during World War II), could take this woman. He had the power but he didn't have the right. Achilles, by our standards, should set aside personal ego and fight for his people. Achilles, by Greek standards, is absolutely right. His first allegiance is to his honor. This conflict between the need of the individual to be sovereign and the need of the community to triumph/survive provides the context for the unfolding drama. *The Iliad* has a political basis but you can read it without giving politics a thought.

Even *Alice's Adventures in Wonderland* rests on a political foundation. It can be read as a glorious fantasy or it can be read as a comment on the powerlessness of a child, of children in society. You don't have to choose—you can read it on many levels, including reading it as a drug trip.

Both *The Iliad* and *Alice in Wonderland* ring true. People read them today with as much pleasure as people derived from them when they were first written. A work lives like that if it is morally true.

You bring to a book your past, your system of beliefs. First, you read a book and answer that book with those beliefs. If you are a student of literature you will study the environment of the writer and then you'll read the book again, setting aside your values. When you've finished the second reading you can engage the writer's beliefs with your own. Reading is an active moral and intellectual exchange. If you aren't reading books that challenge you, you're reading the wrong books.

If you aren't writing books that challenge you, keep writing. It takes years to get there. I know the book I wanted to write, the challenging, lyrical work I dreamed about. You know only the book I wrote. I am acutely aware of the gap between desire and performance. Lash me though you might, you'll never hit me as hard as I hit myself, for only I know the full extent of my failure.

Morality shifts. Infanticide was acceptable to the Greeks. It isn't acceptable to us. Your work will reflect your implied faiths and fears. Without your being necessarily conscious of it, your work reflects your society. Here's an example. Since *The Iliad*, Western writers have treated common experience as comic relief. This attitude depends on a clear class structure in which the superior classes, aristocrats, are assumed better than the inferior classes. When the middle classes began to assert themselves, this shifted. Chaucer in *The Canterbury Tales* presents sympathetic middle-class characters. Some are comic and some are not but none of them is heroic. A great revolution took place on the page. This accelerated over time. Shakespeare used all the classes, to his and our great profit.

Eventually, middle-class people developed the leisure in which to write and what did they do? They wrote about themselves. As the Industrial Revolution wears on, their literature takes over. The middle-class character is not a king or a landed aristocrat but a lawyer or a doctor perhaps. Chekhov comes to my mind instantly. The tendency to present ordinary people (an assumption in itself— are there ordinary people?) as vaguely comic still exists but it isn't as strict a literary convention as it was for a good two thousand years.

When you reject inferiority at the lowest level, you topple the whole structure of dominance. The shift in literature, beginning with Chaucer, reflected real life and, in turn, had an impact upon real life. No longer were kings and queens so important. They were replaced with parliaments or by revolutions. They were replaced on the page. Morally, there's nothing wrong with having a king for your form of government or for your literary hero but as an American I bet you don't write about one.

This struggle for literary representation bubbles over the decades. Today, the lower classes, thanks to programs to get them into colleges, are producing literature. The class in control of the arts, the middle class, finds itself besieged from below. Not only are the lower classes becoming literate, nonwhites and non-Christians have acquired the skills to create English literature. Stick around— the show is just beginning!

As Shakespeare arrived at a creative imbalance between the passing medieval world and the coming modern world (Bacon, Newton, Descartes), so we are at a similar overlap between the nation-state and global interdependence, between men and women, between whites and nonwhites, between the Christian world and science, the Christian world and the non-Christian world, between spiritual concerns and material ones. Like Shakespeare we find ourselves in a time where the future, so thrilling to the nonrigid, terrifies the rigid. Every action has an equal and opposite reaction. Every cultural/social push forward is followed by people organizing to hold back the hands of time. Those men who were willing to kill you if you thought the earth revolved around the sun instead of believing Ptolemy are still here. Those people, like Elizabeth I, who killed their political enemies are here too. Like Shakespeare, you've got to try to make sense of it. You don't have to explain it. He didn't. You need to use it, use every bit of it. This overlap and straining of divergent world views is a gift. Don't ask to live in tranquil times. Literature doesn't grow there.

# EXERCISES

———— ■ ————

The following are exercises which I give my classes. Oftentimes I throw these at the class the minute they're in their seats. The fun of exercise is in putting students on the spot. They can't refer to prepared notes; they have no manuscript to defend. They must, as it were, live by their wits. Usually I allow fifteen minutes to complete the exercise.

## EXERCISE 1: BOOZE, BROADS, AND BOYS

An earlier chapter incorporates one of the exercises I've used for the last fifteen years. How many words and phrases can you find for death and how many for love? Since we've done that, in abbreviated form, try this: How many words or phrases can you find for drunkenness and for sobriety, for women and for men? Now take it a step further and add phrases for drugged states of being. This exercise should show you some of the hidden assumptions of your culture/language.

## EXERCISE 2: THE PARENT GAME

Start by giving yourself imaginary parents. For instance, I'll give myself Shakespeare and Catherine the Great. (Don't want much, do I?) Now take figures known to all of you—such as Don Johnson or Jane Fonda—and give them imaginary parents. Next do this for your characters in a short story or novel you have recently written.

## EXERCISE 2½: THE CHILDREN GAME

Reverse the above. Give yourself imaginary children. Give public figures imaginary children. Put them in a situation where the child, the oldest, has misbehaved. Can you invent dialogue between parent and child? Lastly, do this for your own characters.

The parent game and the children game are attempts to lure you out of the rut of conventional thinking.

## EXERCISE 3: STEALING CHARACTERS

The Fool from Shakespeare's *King Lear* meets Ariel from *The Tempest*. The action takes place after the end of their respective plays. Where are they? Why are they there? What do they say to each other?

You may also substitute two other characters from literature.

(Thank you, Floyd Hurt, for this exercise).

This will help you enter other identities, which is the core of character creation. The Fool and Ariel are already defined. All you have to do is continue their personalities in a new situation.

## EXERCISE 4: MAKE 'EM LAUGH; THEY CRY AT HOME

Exercise 4 starts from this racing block: Wit comes from intellect, humor comes from emotion, and fun comes from imagination. I usually write it on the blackboard.

Wit = Intellect
Humor = Emotion
Fun = Imagination

You must write three paragraphs illustrating each of the above. This exercise is a breeze for some students and torture for others. That's one of the reasons I use it about the fourth week of teaching. Students need to know what their literary temperament is. One's personal temperament may not correspond exactly to one's literary temperament. In other words, you may be the life-of-the-party in person yet dark and tragic on the page.

## Exercise 5: Worry-of-the-Week

Part 1 of the exercise is set in current times. You write down, from recall, current problems in the newspaper and TV news. For instance, earthquakes, secular humanism, stalled economy, and cellulite.

Part 1 helps students see how relative reporting is and how shallow. This is one of those exercises that work best in a class setting because the students read aloud the worries-of-the-week. Usually, what we find is that certain problems recur in everyone's exercise. From this point most people realize they have to go deeper with their research. They've got to go to primary sources. Newspaper and television are not primary sources.

Part 2 can't be done in class. The students must go to the library and read a newspaper that is one hundred years old and repeat the worry-of-the-week exercise. Then they read their discoveries in the next class. We then discuss which worries were legitimate, representing a long-term problem, and which were short-lived or trivial. Since most writers stay in their own time, this becomes a valuable exercise, as it teaches people to put events in perspective.

## Exercise 6: Mildewed Metaphors

Take axioms, sayings, or even corporate names and twist them. For instance: Old soldiers never die, just young ones; Be an Equal Opportunity Offender; General Electric can become Generous Electric.

You can also twist a word. How about *anti-semantic*?

The purpose of this exercise is to have fun and to become sensitive to economy of meaning. You could write a novel based on "Old soldiers never die, just young ones." Learn how to encapsulate ideas. The reason for this is to help you understand the effectiveness of irony and humor. It also makes you think. Taking something old and making something new is what a novel is all about. *Novel* means "new" in Latin.

## EXERCISE 7: VISUAL JOKES ON PAPER

Students must take phrases and make them visually funny
while retaining the recognition of the word or phrase's original
meaning, *plus* the twist which gives it a new meaning.

For instance: Rachel graduated from Vassar *summa cunt
laude.*

Another one: Theresa was *whore de combat.* Lisa was *pièce
de résistance.*

This exercise is different and difficult, so it's one that I let
them do twice. First, they have their fifteen minutes in class. Many
students draw a blank. They have never conceptualized their language as visual. Speaking is auditory. Writing is both visual and
auditory. (It is auditory because most people read with the sounds
in their head. A few don't.) Therefore, you should begin to think of
what you put on the page visually. Can you transmit meaning with
how something looks? Poets play with this better than novelists—at
least, that's been my experience. For the second part of the
exercise I give the students a week to create visual jokes or visual
meaning. It doesn't have to be funny. Students must put their
answers and creations on paper and duplicate enough copies for
the class. People get very excited on the day these papers are to be
passed around. It's great fun.

## EXERCISE 8: SETTING CHARACTERS

Assigned at mid-semester, this exercise takes the rest of the
semester to complete. The information from each student is col-
lated during the last ten days of class and discussed. Students
divide people into three general classes: upper, middle, and lower.
They may then subdivide as they see fit—e.g., rural southern
upper. They must research class-distinguishing features through
library work, personal observation, and interviews. They need to
find out the following things.

1. How is English used?
2. How is money viewed?

3. What is the sense of the future?
4. How is living space utilized? Is it noisy or quiet?
5. If there is leisure time, how is it used?
6. Can you discern attitudes toward sex?
7. Can you discern attitudes toward religion?
8. Is there any way you can estimate alcohol or drug consumption?
9. Are these people accessible, geographically and emotionally?
10. What is the level of formal education? Intelligence, obviously, is native.
11. What aesthetic values can you discern?
12. Do these people have a class consciousness? If they do, how is it expressed?
13. After you have completed the exercise, do you feel you have learned anything? Were your assumptions called into question?

The purpose of this is to get students out of their own backgrounds, to help them enter other realities so they can create a variety of characters.

## EXERCISE 9: SPOOF TITLES

Make up book titles with brief blurbs on the content of the book. These can be funny or serious. Here are some examples: *Writer's Cramp*—a landmark study in menstruation and literary creation; *Fetus to Fossil*—a celebrity biography by a passionate paleontologist; *Orphans of the Norm*—a cry from the heart by one of the leaders of the Gay Liberation Movement; *The Brothers Carry Mats Off*—an inside look at the carpet industry; *Prose and Cons*—a writer's manual written by a former Watergate conspirator; *Fat Chance*—either a diet book or a searing commentary on the career opportunities in El Salvador by an ex-CIA agent; and *Snap Judgments*—a glamour book of photo essays or an exposé of the Supreme Court.

Silliness does seem to take over when students read their exercises. It gets everyone in a good mood.

## EXERCISE 10: THE GREASY SPOON

You have fifteen minutes to write a sketch or short story in which there appears a restaurant place mat that has written on it one of the five following things:

1. A map of the area in which the restaurant is located
2. How to mix drinks
3. Palmistry
4. The Zodiac
5. Our Proud Heritage

## EXERCISE 11: KISSING OFF MA BELL

Have you ever heard of *The Collected Phone Calls of Gertrude Stein?* Writers should learn to write letters and save the telephone for business. Charles Jerry Hannah, a writer, used to bedevil his students with the idea of writing letters. He was right. Any excuse to get you to the typewriter, computer, or pen will begin oiling your brain. The more you write, the better you'll get. You might want to write a letter to a friend before you begin your day's work. I give an exercise in class in which you've got fifteen minutes to write a letter to a public or historical figure. The person may be living or dead. All I care about it that the rest of the class will know who it is. Then we read the letters.

A letter is halfway to first-person narrative but it's in the author's voice.

This exercise is followed by:

## EXERCISE 11½:

You write a paragraph in first-person narrative and then you take the same paragraph and write it in the third person. You'll be surprised at the results of this, especially since you warmed up with your letter.

## EXERCISE 12: NAMES AND CHARACTERS

Surely you've heard someone say that people look like their
dogs. Winston Churchill should have had a bulldog. A fashion
model will slink down the street with a borzoi. This is one of
those cherished notions which isn't really true but isn't really false.

Exercise 12 requires a similar state of mind. People sometimes get the name they deserve and sometimes they don't. However, for the purpose of this exercise, invent names and character
descriptions to fit the name.

Here are some examples:

Ranlet Nottingham — an expert on heraldry at Swarthmore
Odonna Pringle — a waitress at the White Castle
Toxic Worrell — a lawyer loathed by his associates. (You may
use this name only if the story is set after the 1970's.)
Masterpiece Martin — a character free with her favors

## EXERCISE 13:

Give me four good reasons why you should use a tape recorder. Okay, I've heard every one. Now take that machine with its
shiny brown tapeworm and throw it out the window. If you can't
remember what people say, you're in the wrong business. Tape
recorders are for journalists, not novelists. Hear the speech inside
your head. Recall the intervals, the rise and fall of tones. There is a
music to speech and each of your characters should have a different voice.

Of course, if you're determined to use your tape recorder, go
ahead—I'll still talk to you. However, I will fear that you are getting
lazy.

## EXERCISE 14: EXITING HOTEL EARTH

Pretend it's your last day on earth. Tell all the people you
know what you really think of them. Next, take your characters. It's
their last day on earth. What do they say to one another?

*        *        *

I hope these exercises stimulate you as much as they've
stimulated my classes. There is no right or wrong to any of them.
They are designed to alert you to your individual strengths and
weaknesses. They are also designed to help you enjoy yourself.
Writing should bring you deep pleasure. My experience with students is that once they climb down off Mount Rushmore and frolic
a bit, their work improves. They aren't so self-conscious. You need
to relax internally. Again, it's not much different from an athletic
event. If you tense up, become hypercritical of yourself, the work
won't flow. The purpose of these exercises, of this manual, is to
encourage your productivity and your health and also to show you
that success isn't so much sitting up at night as being awake in the
daytime.

# IV
## AD HOC

# THE GOOD, THE BAD, AND THE UGLY, OR READERS, PUBLISHERS, AND CRITICS

Your readers are your best friends. As time goes by you'll find out who they are. No two readers are alike. These distinct individuals put down good money for your work and then spend their valuable time reading it. For the last fourteen years I've been getting packets of mail from my publisher. If I were to average it out I guess it would come to roughly twenty letters per week. Sometimes people throw tomatoes instead of roses, but hell, they sat at their desks and tried to connect with me. I give them credit. I've learned more from my readers than I have from the usual literary sources: other writers, publishers, critics.

The first thing I've learned is that very often people read their book, not your book. They read as though they were writing the book, and of course they would do things differently. Oftentimes these comments can be irritating but just as often they can be instructive. I am never bored at the variety of responses.

The second thing I've learned is that readers love books in general. People write and mention other works that they've read. It's as though those of us in love with literature are part of a far-flung, wildly diverse family but a family all the same.

While the chapter heading said "The Good, the Bad and the Ugly," I don't see my publisher as bad. In fact, I'm one of the lucky ones. I've got a great publisher and I'll celebrate a decade with Bantam Books this year.

However, if you understand what a publisher can and can't do for you, you'll be armed against disappointment. The publisher buys your book and then assumes the risk of printing it, distributing it, and placing it in the bookstores. The publisher is also responsible for editing, advertising, and promotion. If your book sells enough copies to pay off your advance, then you'll earn royalties.

While it's fashionable for writers to bitch about their publishers, it might be wise for you to realize that publishing is a business. Publishing is about selling books, not about nourishing literature. While an editor may burst with pride over a gorgeous piece of writing, the publisher is much more likely to look at the sales figures. It isn't that publishers are cultural illiterates, far from it, but they have to pay you, pay the editor, pay the telephone sales staff (bless those people), pay the art director and graphic artists, pay the typesetters, printers, binders, and mailing costs. They must also pay the newspapers for advertising space; the airlines for tickets if you go on tour, plus hotel and food bills and your phone calls to home; the field representatives, salespeople, the shippers and packers in the back rooms, and God knows who else. Publishing is a business with a slim profit margin. Bantam Books is one of the largest publishing companies in the free world, not counting government publishers (the U.S. Government is its own publisher), yet Bantam's annual report would be a comma compared to General Motors'. In addition, publishing is the only business in which the wholesaler (the publisher) assumes the cost of retail overstock. In the dress business, if a store doesn't sell all its stock, it puts the extra dresses on sale and, perhaps, loses money. In publishing, if the bookstore orders more copies than it can sell, it ships them back to the publisher and gets its money back. I repeat, publishing is a business with a slender profit margin and enormous risks.

Those risks involve you and me. What if our next book bombs? What if we begin drinking and they've got a fat advance out to us with no return? Suing isn't as easy as you think, and why incur legal expenses if there's nothing to recover? What if there's a printers' strike or *The New York Times* goes on strike? Why the *Times*? I speak from personal experience. One of my novels, *Six of One,* was tearing up the country, but since there was no *New York Times* Best Sellers list, I lost bonuses and my publisher lost the publicity advantage of my being on the list. Any business carries attendant risks, but a business that involves public taste involves bigger risks. It takes a certain kind of individual to withstand that nagging insecurity. You've got to be tough. Your publisher's got to be tougher. You've got one book to worry about. Your publisher, depending on size, may have hundreds each season.

Therefore, don't expect your publisher to fawn over you. Don't expect your publisher to understand you.

Do expect your publisher to render you an accounting of your sales every six months. Do expect your publisher to provide you with strong editorial support. (Often your editor is your only connection to the corporate team.) Do expect your publisher to open its accounting books so that you may periodically audit those books. This is an odious and costly procedure but one that is valuable to both of you. Do expect your publisher to target your market. Expect your publisher to give you the advertising and promotion deemed appropriate for your work. Here's where you will often run into disagreements, but while my ego may be in a gaseous state (ever-expanding), my mind is connected to reality. My publisher knows the market. If a book is right for a big tour, great. If not, I try to accept it or hire a publicity agent to push the book. However, publicity agents are not cheap and few of them know books. (Hilsinger-Mendelson is one of the best public relations companies for writers.) Those that do are besieged with work.

If your publisher ever tries to censor you or tell you what to write, walk. No one, not even your esteemed publisher, has the

right to crawl inside your head. They have the right to refuse a book
and that's all.

Publishers are like car dealers—some are good and some are
wretched. Leadership changes. A house that was excellent five
years ago might be crumbling today. A few publishing houses have
maintained solid leadership over the years. It's not my place to
name them here. Ask around. People know. If you hear a bad rap
on a company and you may be about to engage in business with
them, ask your agent or ask a reputable literary lawyer. Most of
these people are in New York City. A few are in Los Angeles but
the orientation there lacks the literary authority of New York. L.A.
does not lack for business sense, though.

If a publisher offers you a contract, talk it through with other
people in the business. Writers are bounced from pillar to post and
we're so underpaid that we often jump at the first offer. You want a
reputable publisher.

Your salvation or your undoing will be your agent. She or he
knows the business, knows reputations both in literary terms and
in financial terms. What good is it being with a big house if they're
deadbeats on payments? You get your check three months late.
They've made interest on that money they've owed you and you've
lost not just that interest but possibly the interest on your credit
cards or whatever credit you've had to use until the check comes.

Your agent knows editors. She knows who is good with comic
writing, who is good with psychological stories, and so on. She will
try to match you with an editor who can work sympathetically with
you. Your agent is your lifeline, your reality check, and your best
friend.

How do you get an agent? Beats me. In 1973, I met mine,
Wendy Weil, through a client of hers. Up to that point about seven
agents had refused me. So had countless publishers in New York
City. I may have been a ragamuffin but I was a clean ragamuffin
and I showed up at publishers' and agents' doors, manuscript in
hand. I tried Random House, Atheneum, Simon & Schuster. I
worked near Crown Publishers (before they became a big house)

and was turned away there. Prentice Hall didn't want me and neither did Macmillan. Open the current *Literary Market Place* and look at the list of publishers. Chances are I was in their front offices in the early seventies, being handed my hat. Downhearted but not defeated, I pressed on. Finally a journalist at *Newsday*, Dolores Alexander, told me to meet her agent, Wendy Weil, at the Julian Bach Literary Agency. As I had little money, I walked from the Village up to the East Forty-eighth Street office. I'd sent her my work. When I first met the woman who was to become my mainstay I thought she was a teenager. She was very quiet. I figured I'd struck out again, but no, she liked my work. She didn't overflow with enthusiasm, mind you, but she actually said she liked my work and she'd put me on her roster. I've been there ever since.

Wendy also liked the work of Mark Helprin, Alice Walker, Judy Rossner, David Bradley, and Laura Furman. We are blessed to have her.

I still can't tell you how I got an agent. I hope you don't have to make the rounds as I did (for years) and I hope you don't get doors slammed in your face. If you don't know of any agents or you live outside of New York or Los Angeles, Poets & Writers (201 West 54 Street, New York, New York 10019) publishes various pamphlets. I think they have an agents list. Poets & Writers exists for you, the writer. Join, and utilize their services.

Your agent presents your work to publishers. She or he prepares your contract and negotiates for you. She advises you on the offer made to you by a publisher. She protects both you and your work as best she can. A good agent knows her business. A great agent knows the business and literature. Developing a writer used to be the province of the editor. While there are a few extraordinary editors out there today, developing the writer is often the agent's province if the agent wants to be bothered. Most often you are left to yourself with no guidance. I'm one of the lucky ones, because my agent sees my work as a continuing body of expression, not as isolated units to sell.

Critics. Ah, yes, I bet you expect me to turn splenetic. I do the work myself, reviewing other people's books, so I work both sides of the street. I expect most writers feel about critics the way a fireplug feels about dogs. However, no matter how many dogs befoul your work they can't really hurt you. Consider this: In the theater a bad review can cripple you. In film it can slow you down, initially. In publishing it doesn't mean a thing. Book critics are powerless.

A book still sells by word of mouth. You can be sliced and diced from the Atlantic to the Pacific and have a runaway best seller. As a critic, does that bother me? No. I recognize that today the critic's function is to fill space in the newspaper. Only the paper's book editor really cares, plus those few of us who love literature. Most big papers are trying to figure out how to gut their book sections because they don't bring in enough advertising.

On my bad days I think of a critic as someone who'd put a cyanide cap in an Easter egg. Tallulah Bankhead said, "Criticism is the distillation of bias and prejudice." The truth lies somewhere between me and Tallulah. Most critics can't create what they criticize. If another novelist writes a review, that's one thing. If the review comes from anybody else, it's hard for me to take it seriously. But then, as you may have gathered, it's hard for me to take anything seriously.

As a writer my feeling is that the critic can help me only when I am writing the book. I don't read reviews of my novels. They're too late to do me any good.

If you're one of those people who reads everything written about you, I suggest you be grateful if your name and the book title are spelled correctly.

Don't be surprised, if you do read criticism, if you are personally criticized through the book. The more controversial you are, the more loaded the reviews. My advice: Eat the chitlins of forgetfulness.

Reading into the tea leaves of literary triumph can be thrilling. Sober up, honey. Tomorrow they'll be on to someone else. Remember in the late 1960's and early 1970's, a flotilla of books was published wherein men attacked their mothers. It was the return of Orestes, obviously not at all certain Clytemnestra was dead. At least Clytemnestra killed Agamemnon (he was such a blowhard, anyway). She did something to incur her son's wrath. By the seventh decade of the twentieth century all a mother had to do was feed her son too much or worry about his health and he was ready to commit literary matricide. Oh, how those books were lauded. Miracles of psychological lamentation they were. Where are they now? Give the same critic the same book today and he'd go "Ho-hum."

Don't believe your own publicity. That way madness lies. You'll soon be stinking in your own decayed ego.

Don't feel responsible for how people misuse your work. Whatever you do can be used against you and probably will be. Keep writing. You're on earth to write, not to indulge yourself in petty squabbles justifying yourself to pissants.

One amazing product of fame, should it come to you, is the number of people claiming to know you. People will emerge who are your long-lost relatives. Old lovers—yes, perfect strangers swear to nights of physical bliss and if you'd just pay them off they'd shut up. It's worse for men. They get slapped with paternity suits. Others fulminate that you've snatched their stories and to prove it they have one sentence on a three-by-five card which uses the word *dumpling*. You started your last novel with the word *dumpling*. Then, too, you will read melodramatic stories told by some unfortunate whom you have wronged in your ruthless climb to fame and fortune. You recognize the face. Yes, it was the shoe salesman at K mart. The reporter also tried to interview the shoe salesman at Gucci's but he refused comment. It's hard to be ruthless when you spend eight to ten hours alone at the typewriter, but you're exceptional. You will find yourself inundated with people who have cast your horoscope. You must consult them immediately because they have the secrets to your future. You will find people at your door, book in hand, because they know you'll be ecstatic to inscribe that book at 6:30 A.M. You'll also find real estate agents relentlessly driving clients by your house when it isn't on the market. "Just looking." These same real estate agents will drop off brochures for you. For some inexplicable reason the houses in these brochures are over $750,000. If the old lovers aren't bad enough, you'll find a steady stream of people applying for the job of new lover. What does it matter that you've been happily married for years?

You will be offered cocaine, booze, and hired sexual partners by certain people desirous of doing business with you. Why do people think that famous people are decadent? I can bear all of the above, but I confess, this one really gets my knickers in a twist.

Well, those are the irritations. The good things are that you should be able to get advances so that you can continue your writing and give up your "make money" job. You might get a good table in a restaurant but don't count on it. Most maitre d's are not interested in literature. You will meet incredible people, which is a joy. What is there to life but people?

Whether fame or notoriety is your fate, put it behind you and put the typewriter in front of you. And put next to your typewriter these words from Albert Einstein: "The only way to escape the personal corruption of praise is to go on working."

# LITERARY VAUDEVILLE: THE ROAD TOUR

Allah be praised. Not only did you sell your book but the publisher has seen fit to send you on the road to promote it. If you think this is going to be glorious fun, you're smoking opium. A road tour is like boot camp without the food.

By now you've read humorous articles by authors regaling you with the mishaps of their first book tours. By the way, no one writes an article like that after the first tour. The mishaps, the miseries, and the mirth are true. As the veteran of four major national book tours plus two minor tours, maybe I can save you some sanity.

Do not grant more than five interviews a day *after* your first tour. On the first tour you have to do everything. Nobody knows you. After that, protect yourself. No rational human being can repeat herself more than five times a day unless she's running for public office. Interviewers ask exactly the same questions. You'll become resentful or scattered or surly. Protect your work by giving five interviews only. Fight with your publisher over this. It's worth the fight.

Demand eight hours of sleep. Otherwise you'll finish your last interview at 8:00 P.M., catch a plane to the next city, get in at 11:00 P.M., get to the hotel at 11:30 P.M. to midnight, and be up at 6:30 A.M. because you've got a morning show to do. You'll be shot before seven days have passed.

Carry food with you. I take apricots, nuts, and dried foods to nibble on because even the best of tour planners can't control my blood sugar.

Tempting as it is to take pills or drink, don't. Every faux pas you commit will show up on television or in print. They'll crucify you.

Don't think you are superior to the people interviewing you, especially the television people. It's true they have not read the book. It may even be true that they have not read the press packet. They are swamped by every third person in America who wants to be on their show. My last book tour I sat in the greenroom with a man who was freeze-drying dead pets, an alternative to taxidermy. (They looked real.) Imagine what your host or hostess goes through in one five-day workweek.

Fiction writers rarely appear on television, because TV interviewers must have something to talk about. They can't talk about your book because fiction, in order to be interesting to the show's audience, must have been read. You're out on the road to get people to read the book. It's a catch-22. The audience hasn't read the book. The interviewer can't interview you. Write a nonfiction book on why carpenter bees will destroy your house and you'll be interviewed. The way a fiction writer gets on television is if s/he is an august personage (in other words, has been around for years and years) and out of sheer shame at being culturally illiterate, the producer lets the writer on just once. The only other way a fiction writer gets on television is if s/he is in some manner, quite apart from literature, noteworthy or entertaining. This includes yours truly, because august personage I ain't.

Should you find yourself facing all of America at 8:00 A.M., remember this: Not many people will recall what you say. They will recall how you look and how you act. (Don't wear all white. It glares.) Your host has ratings to fret over, which means his/her next contract negotiation, which means money. Don't expect the host to make you look good. S/he wants to look good. It's his bread and butter. Well, if you're in front of that camera it's your bread and butter too. Unless a host is personally insulting to you, don't make a fool of him. Merv Griffin was one host who enjoyed bringing you forward and casting the spotlight on you. That's rare.

Expect your host to swallow up your air time with his ideas, ruminations, and eventually a question or two. Don't blow your stack. Whoever he or she is, he has a faithful audience. That's why he's up there. The viewer is loyal to the host, not to you.

People like Maury Povich or Pat Mitchell or Meredith MacRae have passionate fans in the community who line up outside the studio just to get a glimpse of them. The television hosts know how powerful they are. They can read the ratings as easily as their producers. It wouldn't hurt you to read ratings either. They will give you a strong sense of how television works and your small place in the firmament.

Radio also has stars: Diane Rehm in D.C., Joan Hamburg and Dr. Ruth in New York City, and some of the all-night people. In the beginning I underestimated radio. I thought it was only music. As in television, these people know their audience, they know the statistics, they know their sales records, and they know their ratings. Radio people seem to brave controversy more often than their television counterparts. Don't be surprised if you get grilled, nicely. Personally, I have to work harder on radio. I like to look out and see an audience or at least see a cameraperson. I feel very cut off in radio and I'm trying to overcome it. Also, I don't much like my voice, and your radio hostess or host will have a reverberant, lovely voice. I've often wished I could hire Colleen Dewhurst to reply for me when I'm on radio.

If you're going to get blasted, it will be with a print interview. Interviewers for the local newspaper or a magazine may be kind to your face but I often think a miasma of spite overtakes them when they sit down to write the story. We all get gored in print sometimes, so toughen up now. Chairman Mao said, and I paraphrase, that you can judge your success by the reaction against you. Given his hike through China, you might say he was an expert on road tours.

Not all print people are vicious. What I'm saying is: Be wary. You have no protection from them. If they misquote you (this is a given) or if they miss the point of your novel, don't get upset.

Controversy is the stuff of sales. Why deny people the pleasure of a good misunderstanding?

Sometimes I think that print journalists are hard on us because they want to write novels themselves but they haven't gotten around to it. Russell Lynes said, "Every journalist has a novel in him, which is an excellent place for it." Whether or not you agree with Mr. Lynes I bet that quote made you laugh.

Theoretically a print interviewer should be better prepared than a television interviewer. This is not always the case, because the TV person has a backup staff and the print person is usually out there solo. Remember, the print person may have been covering brush fires in Podunk. From the burning bush to you, that's quite a jolt.

Also, print interviewers are accustomed to being lied to. In a funny way their work is like a police person's. They're trying to get the facts and the subject is trying to hide them. Why should the interviewer trust you?

Every now and then you will run across an interviewer who uses a hostile technique. Regardless of the medium, this puts you in a bizarre position. If you lose your temper you divert the focus from the book to you. You aren't selling yourself; you're selling a novel which I hope you're proud of. You want people to read your book, to be moved by it, to think, perhaps by virtue of your provocation. Don't let your ego get in the way of your work. If you are attacked, deflect it. If you can't deflect it, then terminate the interview as quickly as possible and call your publisher. It's a courtesy to your publisher to inform the publicity director of something of this nature. Do it without much emotion, too. The publicity director needs to know your limits as well as the nature of the interviewer. By informing your publisher you're helping the next author.

Whenever I do a tour I keep a log of each interview. I note the effectiveness of the interviewer, the person's appearance, on-camera presence (if TV), familiarity with the material, ability to handle the audience and me. I rate interviewers with an eye not just to how they treat me, but also to what their scope may be. For instance, on my last tour I was interviewed by an intense young man from Fairchild Publishing. I put in my report that he displayed an exceptional grasp of literary material. He had standards; he was more than a flak. Now he may or may not have written a good article about me. That wasn't my point. My point to the publicity director was that whenever she has a writer with difficult or unconventional work, this particular fellow will be good. By way of contrast, an author with difficult content would do badly with a top-forty radio station interviewer (unless that interviewer was quite unusual).

Remember, too, when you're out there, that the people interviewing you are on the job. Chances are there are fifty things they would rather be doing than talking to you. They're getting paid for this. If they aren't professional, there isn't much you can do about it except request your publicity director not to send you back to them should you go on another tour someday. If they are professional, extend the courtesy. Don't waste their time with long-winded answers that are not relevant to the question. Don't waste their time with tales of your family unless that is relevant to your work. Whenever possible give the souls a good quote. Do you have any idea of the dullards they interview daily? They crave something with pizazz and they deserve it. Where is it written that your interviewers shouldn't enjoy the interview? If they have conducted a good interview, tell them so. Don't gush, but compliment them as one professional to another. Don't expect your compliment to mean you'll get good copy. That's not the way the game is played.

Sometimes you may encounter fans. (Don't smile. This isn't as exciting as it sounds.) If people like your work and tell you, that's a fabulous feeling. If they give you flowers or a memento of their regard, be grateful. They went to a lot of trouble to please you. If they ask for more than that, they are over the line. If they are quite young, give them some slack. If they aren't, then try to be polite. I have had overheated lovelies prowling the halls of hotels. I have had to summon hotel guards at all hours of the night to deal with some of these fans. I once had a gentleman fan pose as my driver. Luckily for me, he did get me to my interview but his proposition took my mind off business. I don't think I gave such a good interview after that episode. People do the damnedest things.

Because a person sits down and spends so much time with your book s/he may think s/he knows you. It is an intimate relationship and some people don't realize that you can't be intimate in return. The book was your gift. You have no other gift to give. Fans may adore an athlete, worship a movie star, but they connect to a writer. My fans are very different from my friend Margot Kidder's fans. (For one thing she has more of them!) I've seen people absolutely squeal with delight when they see Margot. I've seen women swoon when James Coburn walked off the plane here in Charlottesville. But when fans see me they don't swoon, they don't squeal; they stare—and then they start talking. If you become the kind of writer who calls forth these heated emotional states (and who knows exactly why it happens to some of us and not to others) my only advice is, be careful. You certainly don't want to be cruel to someone but you don't want to encourage him either. There are a lot of unbalanced people out there. The statistics on sanity are that one out of every four Americans is suffering from some form of mental illness. Think of your three best friends. If they're okay, then it's you.

I couldn't resist.

As to your road tour—break a leg! Remember, it's show business. Don't wish anyone good luck. And one other theater superstition while you are out there in darkest Kansas: Never put your shoes or hat on the bed. Keep those two things in mind and you'll have a great publicity tour.

# HOT CASH
## AND
# COLD COMFORT

Money and writing appear to be mutually exclusive. The average yearly income earned by writers from writing in the United States is $4,775. This inlcudes total income from book royalties, magazine and newspaper articles, motion picture and television work.[1] This is not a happy statistic.

Those whopping advance sums you read about in the gossip columns are usually for a celebrity biography or the occasional topical, sensational nonfiction book written by someone with impeccable credentials, like Shana Alexander. Genre fiction produces one or two writers a generation who can command huge advances. For our time that's Stephen King, Louis L'Amour, and Danielle Steel. Reading these advance sums might make you feel you're missing something. You and the rest of the world. Milton sold *Paradise Lost* for £60. Never measure literature by accounting statistics.

A quarter of working authors earn less than $1,000, according to the Columbia survey. Only 10 percent of authors have a writing income of more than $45,000, and a scant 5 percent earn more than $80,000.

---

[1] "The Columbia University Economic Survey of American Authors: A Synopsis" (New York: The Authors Guild Foundation, 1981).

What do you do? Daily prayer for starters. The second thing you do is never hope more than you work. The third thing you do is find work that can support your writing. Earlier I mentioned the work I did to keep body and soul together. I think physical labor is preferable to quasi-intellectual labor for a writer. Your body may get tired laying bricks but your mind will be free. If, on the other hand, you're an IBM executive, your head will be stuffed with the specialized knowledge relevant to your position. That's a little like renting your life on the installment plan to the corporation. To put it more succinctly, middle-class jobs are exhausting.

You could open a store if you're so inclined but that, too, is time-consuming. Actually, it isn't just the time but the responsibility. The advantage is that you're your own boss. It takes cash or credit to open a business. If you have one or the other I guess it's worth a try, if you can't face physical labor.

The median total family income for American authors is $38,000. Family income represents the total of personal income, spouse's income, and investments separately held. These statistics are from the Columbia University Economic Survey of American Authors. For a writer, two salaries are better than one. Two salaries would seem to be essential unless you're willing to live in poverty. I'm not encouraging you to marry for money but I do think you have a duty to tell anyone who comes into your life that you might not make a lot. What s/he decides to do with that information is up to him or her. I was never supported by anyone while I was learning. I didn't make a dime from my writing until I was thirty. Naturally, I loathed such an unnatural state. With Saint Francis, poverty was a success. With Mizz Brown it was an assault on my senses. There are some people terrified of being comfortable. I am not one of them. If you can find an easier way to become a writer than I did, do it. However, for most of us it's a long, slow grind financially.

Anger comes from unfulfilled expectations. If you marry poor and your mate has dreams of your being a best-selling author— honey, you're in trouble. If you marry for money, you're in trouble. The cynicism inherent in sex for cash—and isn't that what marrying for money is all about?—will infect your work. Be careful.

When you finally do get some money, Uncle Sam will be standing next to you with his hand in your pocket. There's nothing you can do about it initially except curse. I highly recommend profanity when it comes to the Internal Revenue Service. I wish I could figure out a way to starve the flaming lizards. So far I have not been successful but I've learned to lessen the damage. Like most of you, I don't mind paying taxes when they go for our nation's greater welfare. When they go for $750 titanium coffee-pots, I seethe with fury.

If you come from a wealthy background, you know how to protect yourself from taxes. You've had trust funds set up from a time before taxes became so punishing. Most writers do not come from wealthy backgrounds. I don't know what it is but great inherited wealth seems to vitiate creativity. The lower and middle classes provide America with its artists. So chances are when you finally make money you will already be at a disadvantage because you won't be able to protect yourself from the IRS. Our tax laws are making it harder to create new wealth. Old wealth is in little danger. The lower your beginnings on the class scale, the greater the disadvantage.

Here's what you do. Shop around for a good lawyer. Ask your friends. Find a good lawyer before you find a good accountant. Ask your lawyer for five names of accountants s/he recommends. Interview these people and then make your choice. No accountant, no matter how good, can completely protect you from the wild fluctuations of your income. For instance, 5 percent of authors interviewed for the Columbia Survey reported that they earned ten times as much from their writing in 1979 as they did in 1978, while another 5 percent earned only one fifth as much as the year before. There's nothing you can do about this waxing and waning aspect of your income. You can establish an IRA or a Keogh Plan but what you need is someone who understands this fluctuating

pattern. The IRS giveth and the IRS taketh away. How to protect
your assets and earnings will vary each year as our absurd tax
laws change according to the whim of our chickenshit Congress.
That's why you must have a good accountant. Knowing those
changes is her/his job. You haven't got the time to learn all that
yourself. Pay a professional. Don't be penny-wise and pound-foolish.

Get a contract, drawn up by your lawyer, which clearly
states your accountant's responsibility to you. If the person you
wish to be your accountant won't sign the contract, forget that
person. The reason I'm telling you to do this is so you will learn
from my mistakes. I once had a very slow accountant. He was good
but getting him to do the work was like getting an arms agreement
between the United States and Russia. One year I paid more than
$6,000 in late-filing penalties because of him. If I had had a contract
he would have been forced to pay the penalties.

You may be tempted to play the stock market or commodities
market. You're a writer. Where are you going to get the time to be
a biz whiz? If you're making enough to hire a stockbroker, okay.
But they'll churn. (Churn: keep turning over stocks to generate
commissions.) Why buy his Porsche for him? Better to buy one for
yourself. If there's something in the market that interests you and
you have the time to learn about it, okay, but you don't have the
time to learn about everything.

Aside from bonds, people will tell you that real estate is a
good investment. (I am a licensed realtor in the state of Virginia.)
It is, but it's illiquid. It may be hard to get your cash out when
you need it. Commercial real estate offers higher profit, of course,
but greater risk. If you have friends who are respected real estate
brokers, talk to them.

I used to buy run-down houses for a small down payment,
live in them, fix them up, and then sell at a profit. It was hard
work but it kept me going between advances and put a roof over
my head. I also once owned two apartment buildings which were
useful for depreciation but a miserable emotional drain. Since I

couldn't afford to hire a manager, I did the work myself. Getting awakened at three in the morning when it's two degrees below zero because the boiler broke was not my idea of fun. I hated being a landlord but it did enable me to get on my feet.

If you have some cash you can buy a small house, divide it up by floors, and rent them out, dependent on your zoning. The write-offs for real estate remain decent despite the tax changes. It's not as attractive as it once was but it's still worth your taking the time to investigate.

Don't invest in jewels, gold, or silver. Those markets are artificially controlled and the big boys depend on little suckers like you and me to make them rich.

Old cars were another source of income for me. I'd get a good model like a 1957 Mercedes 220S and improve it, drive it, then sell it.

If you lease a car through your corporation that's good for write-offs. You should think about incorporating at some time and your lawyer can tell you when. Whether or not you incorporate will probably depend upon how much you earn from writing and whether it is your primary source of income.

Please don't let anyone pull the wool over your eyes with horse syndications and the like. Unless you know the syndicator and know a fair amount about bloodlines and conformation, you're going to lose your shirt.

Probably the biggest scam in America is life insurance. In order to qualifiy for a mortgage you must buy homeowner's insurance. There isn't anything you can do about that. In many states in order to purchase a car and register the vehicle you must buy car insurance. You can't do anything about that, but you sure can avoid buying a personal life insurance policy. Why give an insurance company your money to invest? They cream off the bulk of the profit and leave you with enough piddling profit to put up with them. You're better off investing your money yourself, even if it's in something like Certificates of Deposit. Anything—I repeat, anything—is better than buying personal life insurance.

Health insurance is just the opposite. You can't have enough of it. In America, a suffering person can be turned away from help because s/he does not have health insurance. God forbid a doctor should treat a patient and not get paid. (I have sympathy for getting stiffed but surely the medical profession can be less barbarous. Where's the line between greed and self-protection?) So get health insurance and pray you never have to use it.

Brown's solution to health care costs: Every day that you are healthy you pay your doctor $2.00. When you are sick don't pay him/her anything.

If you do begin to make money you'll discover the stereotypes about money and artists. People assume you know nothing. They assume you walk around dreaming and probably can't even make change. This attitude might spring from a little bit of jealousy. Artists lead exciting lives. Many other people do not. Envy comes out in a variety of ways, and criticizing people for their lack of financial acumen is one of those ways. It is true that our work is consuming and we can't always take as much time to plan our finances as we would like. That doesn't mean we're stone stupid.

Bankers, not the brightest people to begin with, really don't understand artists. You can educate your banker and you can protect yourself by keeping a file with your banker in which you place copies of your contracts. Bankers do understand contracts, even if they don't understand how you get them in the first place. Most bankers can read the sum written on the dotted line. It's your only hope, because your money will come in strange increments or step deals. (Step deal: You get paid X dollars for a film sale. If the film option is exercised you then get Y dollars.)

You need a line of credit. The contracts will help you get that line of credit. It also helps if you live in the same community for a couple of years. There's a lot to be said for face-to-face contact. Every time you move you have to begin this education process all over again. Also, never expect your banker to give you a break. In the old days character counted for a great deal in the loan process. Banks were smaller then and many were privately owned. Today the president of your local bank is probably one of many local presidents in a vast network of banks. He's as subject to the computer as you are. He may have some ability to use his discretion but don't expect boldness, because he can be fired. It's a pity that banking is becoming so homogenized. Whatever the flaws of the old system, there was room for some creativity and personal judgment. It's all white bread now.

I hope some of this will be useful to you. The only other thing I can tell you is, when you structure your advances, if they're healthy advances—and by healthy I'd say anything over $50,000— spread the money over two years or more if you can. It will help you with taxes and it will also provide a base for you, and that will give you a bit of comfort.

Also, audit your publisher at least once every five years. Every three is preferable if you can afford it. Most publishers have honest accounting departments but you owe it to yourself to open the books. The last audit I ran on Bantam covered four books they published. The cost of the audit was $5,000. That set me back but I learned a great deal about how my novels were earning money and where that money was allocated within Bantam. No business likes to be audited. (Bantam, to their credit, was gracious.) The more you know about how your books perform as a product (it's hard to think this way, I admit) the more it will help you see your strengths and weaknesses. Do you sell more books in the East? in the West? This information shows up in a thorough audit. Also, if you find a discrepancy, address it *immediately*. You will be doing both yourself and your publisher a favor. They don't want a mistake any more than you do.

The last thing I can say to you about money is, you can't take it with you. Never let money control you. I'd rather see someone spend every red cent and relish her/his life than scrimp, obsess, and pinch the pennies. There's something repugnant about a person who centers his life around money. It's only paper and it gets devalued at regular intervals. You're worth more than that.

# MAGAZINE ARTICLES

The advance for your novel may not pay the rent. How else can you earn some money from your writing? So few magazines run fiction anymore that you can't consider them a market. However, you can write nonfiction pieces for magazines.

Each magazine has its own format and style. You'll need to familiarize yourself with them.

Transitions are much more important in a magazine article than in a novel. A transition is how you get to paragraph two from paragraph one. Pick up any magazine and you'll see what I mean. Usually these transitions are forced. I reckon a magazine writer would kill her mother for a good transition.

There are two other peculiarities of magazine writing. One is that you have so little scope. With a few notable exceptions, like *The New Yorker* or *Vanity Fair,* you can hit only one note. Obviously, if you are writing for an academic or intellectual publication such as *Foreign Affairs,* you can be more complex.

The second peculiarity is that magazine editors are just not of the caliber of publishing editors. They—this is a generalization, you realize—lack the patience of book people. They are on faster deadlines, which contribute to this lack of patience.

I can count on the fingers of one hand the times I have been well edited by magazine editors. Usually, they go through your article with a machete. If you do find a good editor, try to work with him/her again, because you can learn something. A good magazine editor shows you how to compress your expression. This way you get more punch. It's a valuable technique to learn.

As to my own magazine writing, I'm either very good or very bad. I have no middle ground in this arena. This may not be true for you but I find that I work as hard and as long on a magazine article as on two chapters of a novel. And the pay is the pits. Magazine salaries have not kept pace with inflation. A writer is paid today the same price for a two-thousand-word article as s/he was twenty years ago. You are actually losing money when you write for a magazine if you are a selling novelist. Cruel, but true. However, a magazine may give you a new audience and that's worth the ghastly pay.

The wonderful thing a magazine can do for you is allow you to express yourself on a subject important to you which you could not express in another format, a novel or a poem.

# NONFICTION AND OTHER LIES

Nonfiction, today, is imperiled by forgetting its function. A nonfiction book or magazine article has one purpose: to inform the reader. If the nonfiction writer possesses a snappy style, the book/story will also entertain.

The spine of every nonfiction work is the vertebrae of facts which the writer must place together in sensible order to get the story to move. Research and investigative reporting are how one assembles the facts which make up any nonfiction work. This is made interesting/difficult because most times there will be parties affected by your book/article who do not want you to get the facts. You will be misled, lied to, and worst of all, morally deserted by your editor! Let me be so clear you can read my lips. Today, editors (most of them) accept and encourage the practice of creating (I emphasize creating) composite characters.

Let's say you are writing a story for a national magazine about drug use among doctors' wives and, more recently, doctors' husbands. You have testimony from fifteen people. In the course of writing your story you may have to toss out the testimony of seven people. Your editor, for the sake of space and a "good story," will tell you to take the remaining eight people and roll them into four composites.

This is immoral.

You say, "Everybody is doing it." I repeat: "This is immoral."

A reader has the right to expect facts. The reader should be able to trust you. If you violate this trust, no matter what your editor says, you aren't just harming your reader and yourself; you are harming me and every other writer committed to telling the truth. You make a mockery of our profession.

If you're dead broke and the editor has a gun to your head, I suppose you could put in the caveat "This is a composite character." I still think it stinks.

I call upon members of PEN International and the Authors Guild to seriously consider this debasement of our profession. I ask you as an individual writer to refuse composites.

And if you are an editor reading this and you are encouraging writers to create composites, what are you—a pimp to a prostitute?

# SHORT
# STORIES

—————■—————

Short stories make me feel claustrophobic. This is a form for which I have little feeling, so I don't think I can say anything constructive. I need a lot of room to develop my plot and subplots, and in a short story you hit only one note. I need a symphony.

A superb short story can be a beautiful thing and I apologize to those of you who love this form. As my mother used to say: "If we all liked the same thing, think how bored we would get."

# PLAYS

I have not written a play since I was eighteen, so I am not qualified to review the process. My natural bent was playwriting and I wrote plays incessantly until I graduated from high school.

What prevented me from continuing in the theater was the heart-wrenching fact that poverty is your reward. As the years have passed, this has become even more true than when I entered college.

So many factors have combined to drive up the cost of producing plays that producers want "a sure thing." (There is no such animal.) This excessive prudence on their part has caused that theater artery, Broadway, to wither to a capillary. Producers have turned to revivals of warhorses like *42nd Street* or to musical spectacles with no story, like *Cats*.

This is not an environment for creative writers. The English language fulfills its greatness in the theater. My generation has been robbed of this expression.

To give you an idea of how bad it is, let me quote Nelle Nugent, who has more Tony awards than I have Montblanc pens. She said to me over breakfast last year: "I can explain to my backers how we lose money with a dud. How can I explain losing money with a hit?"

The power of playwriting is easy to experience. Pick up a copy of a Shakespeare play or one of Shaw's or of anyone you enjoy. Read the play. Shorn of voice, lights, staging, it still rocked you, didn't it? Imagine the voice, lights, and staging now. Even better, imagine your own play.

Apart from the difficulties in getting an original work produced, there is the problem of receiving no advance.

Once you have established yourself in publishing or in film/TV, you will get advances for your work while you are writing. It's a good idea if you want to eat and pay your rent. The theater does not recognize these basic functions. Within the last two years, producers have come up with a tiny advance. As of this writing, it's $7,500.

In the theater the writer is king—but who among us can afford to be king of confetti? That's about all that's left of the theater—little bits of paper thrown in the air.

# SCREENPLAYS AND TELEPLAYS: HOW NOT TO BREAK YOUR HEART

Ungracious reflections are the order of the day for all in the media who write about their servitude. Whether it's Linda Ellerbee or William Goldman, their books, funny as they are, are also frightening.

Is the film business that awful? Sometimes.

Is television the literary form of the black plague? No, it's closer to the yellow plague, actually. You have a better chance of recovering from malaria than from the bubonic plague.

There are good books on how to write screenplays and teleplays and I'm not going to duplicate those efforts. My aim is to help you understand what you're up against should you find yourself in Hollywood.

One little aside, to show you the difference between a novel and a screenplay. A man goes into a urinal. He unzips his pants. He stands there for a moment. Nothing happens. Then he looks down and says, "Oh, shit, I left it in my other pants." You can't make that work in a novel. On screen, with the right actor and the right director, it could work. As a screenwriter you must

learn to live without narrative, and much harder, you must trust
the people with whom you work—of course, they have to earn that
trust.

Yes, you've heard countless horror stories about how this
person or that person ruined a great screenplay. They're true, every
one of them. However, you don't hear the stories about how the
director, producer, or actor made a good screenplay much, much
better. It cuts both ways.

You are accustomed to working in isolation. Your editor sends
you back copy that is blue-penciled and probably full of little
stick-ons too. Film and television people never heard of blue
pencils. You write the first draft in isolation, but after that you
warm your nether regions in meeting after meeting after meeting.
If you are blessed with a good producer, those meetings are
golden. If you're cursed with a bad producer, start bailing the water
out of the boat, because you're sinking.

Here's an example of a bad producer. S/he called you in for a
meeting. You're prepared for a meticulous raking of the script.
What does he say to you? He hands you back your 120 pages and
says, "Give me more sad." (And people wonder why there's so
much self-abuse in the media.)

To give you an idea of the kind of people you might be
dealing with, let me tell you about what happened the day my
mother died. I was writing the second draft of a teleplay, a high-
quality production.

My film agent or someone must have called the producer to
inform the individual of what had befallen me. The producer
phoned me immediately to say, and I quote: "Sorry to hear your
mother died. Do you think you'll still be able to make your
deadline?"

My editor, my literary agent, my film agent, people I had
worked with even in small capacities, sent condolences and flowers.
From the TV producer I didn't even get a 25-cent sympathy
card.

Ill-bred behavior is the norm, not the exception. When you

work with a producer or executive who dimly recognizes that you have a life separate from your mutual project, you are damned lucky. Even then you have to be wary because they'll rewrite you to death.

Did I make my deadline? Yes.

The best rule of thumb I can give you about producers/executives is that they are either at your throat or at your feet.

A good producer is like the owner of a racehorse. The producer buys or breeds the animal. S/he should possess good judgment of the capabilities of a story for visual presentation, just as an owner has a sense for a horse's potential. The producer then raises the funds and hires the team to develop the project. You're the trainer, the director is the jockey, and the actor is the horse. You're part of a team. That's what is so different about media work: breaking down the isolation.

Unfortunately, most producers are too cheap to have the writer on the set for the first week's shooting. Writers and actors are natural allies. Separating us is foolish. Having the writer on the set can save an actor time, and time means money. Each can help the other sharpen character. If quick changes are needed the writer is there to keep the characters *in voice*. What happens is, the producer gets tight as the bark on the tree and dumps everything onto the head of the director. Some directors like this. They're born masochists. Also, they think they're in control when the writer's out of the picture. What they are is teetering toward exhaustion. If a director does not have an ego as inextinguishable as JFK's flame, progress can be made.

Without the writer on the set, the director substitutes dialogue or lets the actor do it. That's like letting the anesthesiologist make the first cut on the patient because you're trying to save surgery costs. Any solid film or TV writer can hear when the dialogue's going flat. Each character should have his/her own speech pattern as well as his/her own motivations. My experience has been that most producers and directors have tin ears. They might know good dialogue when they hear it but they can't reproduce it.

So, while film and television breaks down isolation to a point, you're often out in the cold. The only people you see are the producer and his/her staff. Maybe, if the producer is gracious, you'll have one meeting with the director and a few of the actors.

I should also tell you that I like most directors. Aside from having a tin ear, they seem to me to have far more virtues than faults. Like the writer, the director sees the entire movie. Unlike the writer, the director sees it in technical terms. Lawrence D. Cohen once said to me: "A screenplay is a strategy for a movie." The writer is the general back at headquarters. The director is the officer with his ass on the field, the supreme tactician.

Still painting with broad strokes here, let's switch the canvas to television. A teleplay is locked into a rigid format much like a sonnet. Once you learn and accept the format, you can say anything. In other words, you must learn the pleasures of restraint. You can wander in a novel; you have luxury akin to the wealth of Louis XIV's court. You can develop minor characters. You can take a side trip off the main story line. You can describe the chiming of a cathedral bell in three pages. You can't do this in a screenplay and you have even less room to maneuver in a teleplay.

Both forms demand that you stick close to a single path. Out There they call it the "arc of the story." God, I hate that kind of talk, but we both might as well get used to it. The buzzwords of film and TV are almost as bad as the buzzwords of psychobabble. At any rate, you write in primary colors. In a screenplay you might be able to offer us secondary colors. Never with TV. TV is a reductive medium, and if you work within its self-imposed limitations—I am saying they are not natural to the medium; they are imposed by the people running the medium—you still have a tiny hope for creativity. The average television show is written so that a fourth grader's mind can grasp it. Before you turn up your nose, remember that Shakespeare included something in his plays for the pit. Also remember that Shakespeare could put something in for the "smart set," too. So far that hasn't happened in TV.

What about censors? Film has a ratings board. It's one of those compromises which backfired on the people who developed it. Give a movie an R rating and they run in from the hills to see it. However, a rating isn't the same as censorship.

Television is infested with censorship. Each network has a "broadcast standards" department and a "compliance and practices" department, with the authority to review every script and pass judgment on it.

I co-wrote a show called *I Love Liberty.* (Rick Mitz, Norman Lear, Richard Alfieri and Arthur Seidelman were the other writers.) I created a valedictorian who falters in the middle of her speech. She admits she isn't sure the future is so rosy. One of the sentences she was supposed to say was: "What about Viet Nam and Kent State?" The censor demanded I remove this. Why? The news covered those events. Viet Nam was in American living rooms. Why not use that sentence? Well, *I Love Liberty* was prime-time entertainment, not news reportage. According to the censor, *Viet Nam* and *Kent State* are loaded words. We can't have these words on a show that's entertaining. I must replace them with the word *turmoil.* The producer, Norman Lear, was fighting to get the show on the air. He protested but we eventually accepted the censor's demand. If you ever see a rerun of that show, you will not hear the words *Viet Nam* or *Kent State.*

Censorship can be unwittingly funny. Have you watched what I call theme shows? These are often brave attempts to dramatize what's happening to us, shows about drug abuse, child abuse, incest, and the like. Bless the people producing these things. You're probably getting an idea of how hard they must fight. Well, the censors cling to these scripts like ticks on a dog. The solution to this has been that in almost every "theme" show you will see, a therapist appears in the fourth act, if not before. That's right, folks. Rub a little therapy on it and that nasty rash of incest just disappears. Do I like it? No. Do the producers like it? No. (Don't

underestimate network executives. They have tremendous intelligence but so few of them have any real power—or guts.) Do the
sponsors like it? I expect they do. It's a little "safer." Do the
censors like it? You bet. Do therapists like it? Hell, yes. It's got to
be bringing them business.

If you ever write one of these shows (mine was *My Two
Loves*, with Reginald Rose as co-writer) you smack that therapist
in there. It's a formula and once you know when and where to look
for it, an unintentionally funny one.

By now you're getting the idea that television is nuts. It is. It's
also fun. It's faster than film. It's freewheeling in some ways that
film isn't. Writers can be part of the producing process much more
easily than in film. This depends on the producer, but my experience has been that the producer will usually let you make the
rounds with him/her if you express interest. You can also be on
the set. Because it's shot faster, your salary isn't going to mount
up, so the producers are sometimes generous.

Everyone in television knows the medium's limitations. We
joke that we are paid highly and bullied frequently—but nine out
of ten of us get a charge out of the medium itself. There's
something intoxicating about knowing your program could reach
200 million Americans in one single night as a shared experience.

The secret of television is very simple. People don't turn off
their sets when they're angry. They turn them off when they're
bored. My friend Rick Mitz, another writer, came up with that
statement one cold Virginia night when we were sitting around the
fire congratulating ourselves on our temporary escape from Los
Angeles. But it's so true it hurts. What hurts even more is the
networks' inability to embrace that truth.

Television is caught between a rock and a hard place, to use
an old phrase. Like other forms of the media—newspapers, magazines, film, radio—television is a business, a community service
(lately much forgotten), and lastly a maverick industry. A maverick
is an animal that cuts out of the herd. If you own a carpet business
you can count inventory, count sales, hear the pitch on next year's

colors and technical improvements. While the carpet industry has
its rough moments, it is still quite safe compared to television or,
by extension, film. In order for the media industries actually to
work, produce, reap a profit, they must create. Therefore they must
employ or seduce creative people. They've forgotten that. Television
networks are stocked with number-crunchers, people who desperately want guidelines and safe answers. It's one reason the television you are looking at today is not nearly as exciting as the
television of 1951. A completely different kind of person spins his
web in the network corridors. Bright, attractive, looking for the
main chance, the new breed (my age and younger) talk a good
game but they are afraid to take risks. Television and film demand
that people at all levels have brass balls or brass ovaries. Unfortunately, we live in the reign of the eunuch. This is going to change
only when a network president 1) stands behind his/her creative
staff and 2) goes into battle with his "bosses," the original men in
the gray flannel suits. Don't hold your breath.

The networks are not all the same. CBS carries the flag of
William Paley. The other networks have grown away from the big
men who founded them or guided them soon after birth. Think of
networks as European countries. They form a geographic entity but
France is different from Germany. I think of CBS as Germany right
after Bismarck. Its unification is suspect but its power is intact.
NBC is like France; it has a commitment to style. Maybe I'm the
only one who has noticed this but NBC shows have a "look" and
it's an expensive one. (Think of the old days in film. MGM had a
rich, textured look. The shots had such depth of focus you fell into
the screen.) ABC is like Italy. ABC has moments of shimmering
brilliance allied with total trash. When Thomopoulos ran ABC it
was like the Rome of the Caesars. It seemed nothing could stop it.
The weaknesses of the Empire have been revealed, but television is
cyclical. ABC has nothing to gain by imitating the other two
networks. If someone at the top realizes that and will take chances
with new programming, then ABC will be on top again until it
grows lazy with success.

What you will face as a writer in television is that you will be forced to be all things to all people. That's why the shows are so dull. An aside: Prime time is the hours of the early evening when the whole family watches TV—notice that the statistics on families have changed drastically in the last ten years, if we are to believe our Census Bureau, yet TV is slow to pick up on this. Oh, sure, there are more shows with single-parent families but there is almost no recognition that there has been a quiet rebellion, or a change determined by economics, against the nuclear family. Programmers for prime time still think it's the fifties and sixties in that respect. Anyway, prime time homogenization should have freed the networks to appeal to fragmented audiences at nonprime times. Networks shrank from the giddy possibility of creating shows for, say, 11:00 P.M., that were written in a twelfth-grade vocabulary. It's still baby talk on the tube. Maybe the themes are more adult, but the style pitches to the lowest common denominator. This, more than anything else, will drive you crazy. There's nothing wrong with writing for people of lower educational or intelligence levels but there is also nothing wrong with offering sustaining fare for those who are ready for more.

If you land in TV, be wary. You can burn out fast. Keep a part of yourself for yourself.

Film people, in general, believe they are superior to TV people. If that is so, then why should going to the movies be a form of punishment? Can you list, for the last calendar year, ten American films that you thought intriguing, passionate, and perhaps even funny? (Comedy is more difficult than drama, so I don't expect too many comedies on your list.) If you come up with ten or more, your standards are lower than mine. I find most movies unconvincing. I'm not even quibbling about the theme; I'm talking about the script. You know, those 120 pages you need before anything else happens? I look up at the screen and I don't see people I can identify with, stories that hit home (operative word, *home*) and are well constructed. What I see are star movies or kid movies. Kids deserve their own movies. I deserve mine.

Wake up, Hollywood. There really are adults in America who love film.

You go into the theater and what do you get? A star vehicle. If it's Clint Eastwood or Paul Newman or Anne Bancroft, I know they might take a chance, give me a character that's a loser or has a touch of evil. That's why Jack Nicholson is so fascinating. It isn't that he plays evil characters but rather that he understands each human is capable of evil as well as good. Without the potential for failure, for evil, for petty spite, there is no potential for growth, redemption, true emotional change. But usually what do we get? We get Robert Redford or Barbra Streisand, who start out good and get better. It's Crusader Rabbit time. The tension in these star vehicles is manufactured. You don't believe it because you know Robert Redford isn't going to fail. I'm glad to say Streisand's recent film *Nuts* represents a departure from this norm.

There are many good books about what has happened to the studio system. If you read them you'll understand how the star as producer came about historically. I don't have room for it here. And by the way, I admire Robert Redford and Barbra Streisand as artists. My purpose is not to make fun of them. My purpose is to reveal what happens when a system gets very out of whack. The material these people and others like them are choosing (and the studio is backing) may make them look good, may make them even richer than they are, but too seldom are they deepening themselves as actors and actresses. Time to return to their talent.

Being a writer for a feature film is like being a cowboy. You sign on until the herd gets to Kansas City. The studio has no loyalty to you. The producer has no loyalty to you. The actors have no loyalty to you. Naturally, they want you to do your best but they aren't connected to you. You rarely see them.

In the old days, writers worked at the studio. Like stars, they had contracts—not as lucrative but still, a steady job and the sense of being part of a company. You drove your car on the lot. You walked to the writers' building. You ate in the commissary. You knew people and they knew you. If you were a trainer, wouldn't you want to know how high your horse could jump? In those days you did. You knew that Clark Gable had a limited acting range but within that range he was golden. You knew Agnes Moorehead could act rings around most people in the business. You knew George Cukor would direct your work with refinement and wit. You knew Howard Hawks, very good, was a different kind of director. You were part of a family—it fought, made up, and fought some more. Now, honey, all we do is fight and we aren't even family.

Maybe it's me. I'm a Southerner. I like belonging to a group. Even if I got a two-picture deal at Fox, I'd never really be part of the studio. I think people need to belong. They need connections. They need to work with people with whom they can build relationships. When we know one another we invent shortcuts. Things don't have to be explained. Now, we don't know one another, and every film project starts at Square One. It's difficult to give your best—but try. Film is a glorious medium. It's worth the suffering and braving the shortsightedness of studios that have dismantled their entire creative populations.

Film allows you windows into your characters. In a film the audience has precious moments in which they catch the character off-guard. They see what others (in the film) do not. Yes, you can write that in a novel but it's not the same as seeing it. The textures of faces give you a new weapon. In your novel, the face is imagined. The first time in a film that you see a main character's face should be memorable. I like to obscure the face so it emerges out of a shadow or it's turned up to the viewer. That's always a powerful moment and the viewer never forgets the face or that first impression—the first vital clue to inner character. What a gift that camera is! You have drama without a single line.

In film everything is relative. This is not quite as true for a novel but a film is a contained experience. The viewer is imprisoned for the one and a half to two hours it takes. With a novel, readers have the freedom to determine how they will accept it. Film makes the audience passive. They are stuck in their seats.

So within this short span of time you must create a self-contained world. In film you cannot know pleasure if you don't know pain. It is possible in a novel not to play opposites. A novel frees you conceptually but you are tied to narrative. A film frees you from narrative but has a narrow conceptual scope. It's a clean trade-off.

The image is primary, not the word. Hard on the writer's ego, that one.

No show should strain the limits of the human bladder. Fortunately a novel can, which is a big advantage over film. The reader might put the book down and go to the bathroom. Or the reader might even take the book into the bathroom. In fact, many books are read in the bathroom. This is a sobering statistic upon which I prefer not to dwell.

The worst drawback of film and television is that writers are not respected. In the theater you are the king. In publishing you are a demigod. In film and television you're the hired help.

The second worst drawback of working in film and TV is that most producers' and studio executives' references are other films or TV shows. Titles such as *Casablanca* will be tossed at you. Carole Lombard and Debra Winger will be mentioned in the same breath. This is confusing and stupid. It means the ideas from the very beginning are derivative.

Your references are real life. One of the major communication problems I have in the industry is trying to get a producer or executive to envision a real character. They'll kill you with inappropriate comparisons.

When I work I want to be original. I don't mind adapting a book to a film, but given my druthers, I want the whole show to sparkle with life. I want it to be mine. I long for the day when the idea is mine too.

This derivativeness, this fear or inability to be original, may come from many sources. I don't understand them but let me relate a famous Hollywood story and leave out the name. A powerful head of a huge company was talking to his staff about what the public wants. He referred to the public as "those people we fly over."

Enough said?

If you work in these fields, fasten your seat belt and reorganize your ego. Otherwise, you'll live on Rue Regret. And don't whine. Actors can whine. Writers cannot. Anyway, why waste your time in melodrama? There's enough real pain in being yourself.

Will working in these fields destroy you as a novelist? That's individual. The focus on plot which exists in film and television has helped me when I return to write a novel. Like so many southern writers, I can digress. Working in the media has tightened my novels and strengthened my ability to weave subplots in and out.

The emotional battering you take will hurt you but not the actual writing process—at least, that's been my experience. Don't be afraid. Try it once. No one's got a gun to your head. If you don't like it, forget it. We each learn to face and survive the conventional humiliations of professional failure. What have you got to lose? If you don't take chances you'll fall on your behind anyway. You might as well fail on your own terms and occasionally succeed as well.

If you can become detached from your work but not indifferent to it, you'll flourish in the media. If you can be passionate about your novels but not single-minded, you'll flourish in publishing.

You need a TV/film agent. Oftentimes your literary agent will have a tie-in to a West Coast film agency. My first agent was Nancy Hardin, who went on to Paramount and then on from there. Maggie Field inherited me from Nancy. We truly enjoyed each other's company. Maggie then went to the other side of the fence—buying, not selling—by going to Walt Disney Productions. (After a few years there, she started her own agency.) Stu Robinson of Robinson-Weintraub-Gross then became my agent and he's a dream, really. He calls me at least once a week with a batch of new offers and he knows the players, so his advice has proven blue-chip.

A literary agent can be a film agent but I think the two fields are so specialized you are better served by having two different agents.

There's a lot of false snobbery on the part of writers who do not get the siren call to Hollywood. You'll hear dire predictions that writing for film and TV will destroy you as a fiction writer. Maybe it will and maybe it won't, but let me quote a Hollywood veteran, Gore Vidal: "Teaching has ruined more American novelists than drink."[1] It seems to me there are better things to worry about than Hollywood.

[1] *Oui* magazine (April 1975).

# SHORTHAND: NOVEL VERSUS SCREENPLAY

Off the top of my head, I've listed what I think the major differences are between a novel and a screenplay. See what you think.

| *Novel* | *Screenplay* |
|---|---|
| 1. The word is primary. | 1. The image is primary. |
| 2. Can have a broad conceptual scope. Can have complex themes over which a plot and many subplots are woven. | 2. A narrow conceptual scope. By necessity the form is simple. Usually there is room only for a major plot and one subplot. |
| 3. The work of a single, unified consciousness. | 3. The work of fragmented consciousness or, if exceptionally good, the work of blended consciousnesses. |
| 4. Narrative is a major tool. | 4. Narrative does not exist although you can make a weak case for the technique of voice-over. |
| 5. You can use inner monologue. | 5. You can use inner monologue only if you use voice-over. |

6. No time restraints.

6. A film should not exceed the limits of the human bladder. Most films aim at ninety to one hundred and twenty minutes.

7. Readers are interactive with the work and usually quite intelligent. You can write "up" if you choose.

7. While a viewer may be somewhat interactive with the material the usual state is a passive one. Some viewers are intelligent but film is aimed at a broader audience so often you must write "down."

8. Can be politically red-hot.

8. Usually safe and bland. On rare, rare occasions a film will be highly political.

9. The writer is often under financial stress. The pay is low.

9. Once a writer is established the pay is quite good.

10. While you reach a smaller audience your work, if exceptional, has a long-range effect over many cultures. Think of Sophocles, Tolstoy, Yourcenar, etc.

10. You reach a huge audience but the work, except in rare instances, has a short-range effect and then is put aside or forgotten.

11. There is a long and great tradition.

11. The medium is barely a century old and while we have a "language" of film there is much to be invented.

12. A novel can only be subverted if the author consents to that subversion.

12. A film can be subverted with frightful ease and the writer is helpless. This is especially uncomfortable in times of political repression.

13. A novel is relatively independent of technology. Once the book leaves your house

13. This art form is completely dependent on technology and that technology is outra-

the mechanics of producing it are still fairly simple. If worse comes to worst you can run it off on a mimeograph machine.

geously expensive.

14. A reader can carry a novel anywhere and read it at any time.

14. A viewer must go to a theater at a proscribed time or have the equipment, e.g. a VCR in his/her home.

15. Usually, the writer has plenty of time in which to develop the novel.

15. The writer is almost always under time pressure which can result in the work not being fully realized.

16. Your readers will identify with you and look for other books by you.

16. The viewer rarely if ever focuses on the writer; the focus is on the actor. Few viewers, only the sophisticated, even care about the director or the producer.

17. Slang will date first. By date, I mean show the age of the book or even make the work appear ridiculous.

17. The score will date first.

# A CIRCUMFLEX ACCENT: BENDING BACK

From the time I started gathering my notes of twenty years to write this book, until this page was put to the typewriter, one year has passed. I had to squeeze days from my novel and screenplay schedule to write this, because, as I am sure you have figured out, a manual does not bring the writer much money. So I worked at other jobs to make the money to write this book.

This little chapter contains the odd thoughts and developments of the last year.

I finished a screenplay for White Cap Productions (an independent company which had a deal at Twentieth Century-Fox) which is called *Sweet Surrender*. What is currently happening to *S.S.* as I think of it, will give you some insight into the film business. Twentieth praised the screenplay but decided they didn't want to make the musical. Now don't ask me why they said lovely things about the writing. Obviously, I don't believe a word of it but I can only go on the information given to me. So the project is in "turnaround." That means the producer, White Cap Productions, may shop it around. If another studio wishes to make this movie they will pay Twentieth their preproduction costs incurred to date and then go on and make the movie. Do I have any special feelings about this? No. I learned years ago to let my work go, once it's out of my typewriter. When you work in film and television it's a bit like building a car. You sell that car outright. If they want to drive it off a cliff, that's their business. Of course, I'd love to see the movie get made but it's out of my hands.

As soon as *S.S.* was finished I hired on at Universal to write a movie called *Table Dancing*. As I write this I am trying to wrestle some agreement out of the studio and the producer concerning the scene-by-scene breakdowns. Now I don't need scene-by-scene break-downs (the bare bones of the plot, literally scene by scene, shorn of dialogue and with only the main emotional points touched) but I learned that most executives do. It calms their nerves and allows them to think they are contributing to the writing process. Natu-rally, they have suggestions concerning these scene-by-scenes. Usually the suggestions are vague and useless because the poor people are overloaded with maybe twenty-five or more stories, scripts, films at a time, in various stages of production. I am never offended by the bland and often indecipherable suggestions. At least they took the time to think about the project and they feel the better for it.

Protocol dictates that the studio executive does not call the writer. The actual producer calls the writer with the suggestions. While I don't like this kind of telephone tag, there is a reason for it. As stated above, the studio executive is on overload. Save the man or woman that phone call. Secondly, the producer should care about this project in a much more personal way than the studio executive does. Therefore it falls upon him or her to deliver the blow, the flowers, the news, whatever. The problem is, you never really know what the studio executive said. So every writer in film and television is working on flawed or partially distorted (usually to save your ego) information.

As regards *Table Dancing*, the real test is the first draft. I can write scene-by-scenes until I'm blue in the face. It doesn't mean a thing. (If you are a studio executive reading this, I apologize for this unwelcome revelation.) What counts is the first draft and only the first draft, because that's when the material breathes. The characters walk and talk and make their own decisions. I have yet to follow any scene-by-scene breakdown I have ever written. I use it but then I depart because the characters take over. It's the joy of discovery, the magic of creation. And it's always better than the scene-by-scene breakdown, despite the flaws. So I will start the first draft of this, probably next week. Even though no one is very relaxed about the scene-by-scenes, eventually they will come to this conclusion: "What the hell, we paid her—let her write." And write I will.

Now I don't mean to sound cynical. And I don't mean to pretend that scene-by-scenes aren't helpful to me. They are. But I look at them as the roughest kind of map (and the map is never the terrain!), whereas the studio executive wants everything pinned down even to the street names. Naturally, you can't do that. But you must remember that producers and studio executives are nervous and this gets passed on to you. (The real trick of writing for Hollywood is in resisting everyone else's nervousness.) These men and women have good reasons to be nervous. First off, they have no job security. (That's okay—neither do I. Get tough, brother.) Secondly, they have been stiffed so many times they are wary. Simply to work with an individual who delivers on time is really a big deal in the movie business. To work with an individual who isn't a flaming neurotic is almost beyond an executive's comprehension. Thirdly, everyone wants something from the executive. That means they are blatantly and subtly bombarded every minute of their working day and often their social life is likewise affected. After a time, this has got to twist your feelings about people and make you either hard or suspicious. Fourthly, they must show a profit to the shareholders. This puts them under tremendous pressure to produce short-term profits. The loss, as you have figured out, is to long-range planning and the development of new talent and even new markets. I wrote in the chapter on screenplays how the lack of creative continuity has affected writers. It ultimately affects the whole studio.

As of this writing I am sad to report that even Universal is no longer a "full-service" studio. You cannot take a project from embryo to birth to "graduation from high school" anymore at any of the studios. The last to dismantle their full creative and technical team was Universal. Yes, the sound stages are in use and the technical people still mingle with the actors and the producers, but these projects are often not "in-house"—the stages are rented by other companies, the teams are hired for the project, and the post-production takes place somewhere else.

Using the excuse of the value of real estate (i.e., let's sell off our back lot to developers), or whatever excuse a studio wants to use, only further demonstrates the short-term approach that infects the whole business. If the real estate is worth so goddamned much, then sell it and build another studio in Indio or Charlottesville, Virginia, or North Carolina (which De Laurentiis did). But don't shatter your creative team. Tie those people together and tie them into the corporation through shares. If I'm a shareholder I might view a project differently from the way I do as the hired gun. I'm not saying that any of us wants to screw the studio but when you are not connected, what motivates you is the story and your ego and, I suppose, for many, the money. If you are tied, I think there has to be a shift. You still have an ego, but surely you would care about the company as an entity, and I think, perhaps in tiny ways or large ones, that will affect performance.

Sir Henry Irving (1838–1905), the first English actor ever knighted, was an actor/manager who changed the shape of English theater both through his performances and through his drive to upgrade the entire production process down to the last costume. He said that theater "must be carried on as a business or it will fail as an art." I believe this passionately and I wonder why those executives don't learn their business. Film, television, and theater are unique. You cannot prepare for them even by running a huge and successful distributorship of films or a movie-theater chain. You can only prepare by submitting to the process itself.

Intrinsic to film and television is the hard fact that there are no easy answers. Content changes. Public moods shift. Technology alters marketing—think of the VCR explosion. If you can't take that insecurity, you're in the wrong business.

You'd be shocked to discover how many executives don't understand the nature of film. They want the business to conform to other models and they spend a lot of time (your time, too, since you watch the result) trying to put a square peg in a round hole. If I could run not the world but just Hollywood I wouldn't promote people unless they'd spent a few years in the field. Let them write, direct, act, or try. Let them work on location. Let them learn how and why this industry is so special and different. However, I do not run Hollywood, so we can look forward to more slick fellows in business suits with M.B.A.'s or law degrees, climbing the corporate ladder. Who knows, maybe even those guys will learn eventually. One can hope.

Well, I don't expect executives to be creative but I do expect them to have courage. If you hire creative people, then trust them. Don't second guess them or wear them out by forcing them to explain to you in analytical terms what can only be approached by synthetic (as in synthesizing) intelligence. As a woman, I find it very embarrassing to be in a meeting and realize I'm the only one in the room with balls.

What has also happened to me in this field since I began writing the manual is that I sold my first sitcom. It's called *Nora's Ark* but I don't know what it will finally be called. Film and TV titles change frequently. The story is set in a southern city's SPCA. Gross-Weston Productions optioned it, which gave me a little money and a little time to refine the idea. So their company and my company then sold the story to Fox Metro. I have no idea if you will ever see this. But I do know I will write the pilot and supervise the show if it gets picked up. Never having written sitcoms, I'll have great fun with this because I love to learn. The other excitement is that this is my baby. As years go by I'm sure the experience of *Nora's Ark* will be worth an addendum to this manual. I promise to tell all!

Since this is the circumflex chapter, the catchall, let me tell you briefly what has motivated me toward film and television. I believe in the process itself. I want, someday, to be able to write a

cycle of feature films or films for cable that are my Brandenburg
Concertos. I have had, since I was quite young, an idea that
connects six separate stories. Like the music, each story is different from every other story. You can "hear" one piece and not need
to "hear" the others. But if you "hear" the entire cycle, taken as a
whole, then you will realize that a single guiding theme is at work.
I may never realize this dream. But if you want to know why I do
what I do in this business, it is so I can finally make enough
money for other people that they will just give me that slender shot
at creating what I long to create. As is so typical of me, much of
this material is funny/provocative. I write elsewhere in this manual
that I think comedy is deeper than tragedy. Not every film will be
funny but there is that joy of life, that reaching out that signifies
my work and, I hope, myself.

The method of this dream—and this is the hard part—is
repertory. I crave working with the same team of actors. I have said
creativity comes from trust, and look at Ingmar Bergman's work,
look at Fellini's work—they're a form of repertory and the trust is
enormous. It shows in every frame. For the record, I love actors.
They are the most abused people in the business and while I can
burn at their insecure antics I understand where that behavior is
born. These people with their fragile, godlike gifts are your life-
blood. Don't make fun of them. Don't threaten them—they get
enough of that elsewhere. Don't indulge them if you can help it. Do
applaud them. Do challenge them—make the roles tough; force
them to sweat and cry and grow. Bring out the best in them, even if
you have to beat it out of them. Most actors are using 20 percent of
their gifts because they haven't been challenged to use more. And
above all, do cherish them.

Now, one last aside on film and TV. Shows are made and shot
from a male P.O.V. (point of view). Currently, there are a rash of
pouty, sultry, intense men on the screen. I think this interests
teenaged girls but I'm not sure that type of man interests adult
women. I'm all for youngsters' having their sex symbols, but I'd
like mine. This brings up the uncomfortable subject of what is

going on with men vis-à-vis men in the business. Most writers, directors, and cinematographers are heterosexual men. I can vouch for this. But I am beginning to wonder if their portrayal of other men is not subconsciously homoerotic. I don't even want to talk about women in film—that's a book in itself and Molly Haskell has written one on the subject, *From Reverence to Rape.* Why isn't anyone talking about men? The obvious sexuality of men in most films is both one-dimensional and, I hope, false, because it's boring!

I want to see men from my P.O.V. I want restraint, complexity, and muscular bodies. (Miss Brown has her muscle fix, which is probably as bad as the big-boob fix of so many men. But I do think women adore beautiful bodies.) I want to take the camera and travel over that actor's body the way my eye reacts to a man when I view him for the first time. If ever we needed yet another good reason for having more women in power in film, that's the reason. How are men ever going to know what we really feel/think if we don't show them? On a more venal level, how are men going to know how to attract us without this information? I ask you, men in film, what are you so afraid of? If I am equal to you in power, does that diminish you? Or are you so uninterested in women's P.O.V. that you can't be bothered to let us show it? The funny thing is, I'm not mad. I'm confused. Why would any man who loves women, wants them in his life, refuse knowledge of them? See, this gets back to hidden homoeroticism in film. I know there is a connection of the fear/ignorance/whatever of women to the homoeroticism. However, I am not the person to unravel this knotted ball of twine.

Would it upset men if they found out we weren't different? Are we? Aren't we? Damned if I know. I only know I have stories inside me that want to get out. I think other women and men want to act them. I think plenty of creative women are facing this same dilemma. I don't know if any of us has a pat answer, but I think we have each been rebuffed at times in our careers because we did want to show the women's P.O.V. and it was upsetting to the male executive we talked with, or the producer. Are men afraid we will mock them? We will, but we'll also mock ourselves if we're any good. Might it be a terrible shock to discover we actually love men? Maybe love is harder to bear than criticism.

Does this mean I want to direct? Not that anyone cares but me. I'd like to try. I know it's hard to break into it but who knows? I'm not dead yet. Anything can happen.

# Change Reality; Don't Abandon It

---

Living tissue connects ideas and generations. Life is a conversation between the dead, the living, and the unborn—between all that was and all that can be. Writing preserves this exchange and enables you and our generation to reach beyond the limits of our physical existence. What would our lives be like if Aristophanes had not written *The Birds* in 414 B.C.? Would we not be impoverished souls if Tolstoy had decided writing was too difficult? Every time a person puts pen to paper s/he bids for immortality. Or at the very least, she makes a bold try to reach out to those she will never see or hear. Writing is a communal art. It brings us together over centuries and over national boundaries.

Naturally, only the greatest writing breathes at this exalted level. However, it's hard to discern what's great and what isn't among our contemporaries. The ticking of the clock will weed out the great from the good, and the good from the bad. You can't fret over the position of your work. You can only produce and hope that a bit of it might prove worthy or useful. Since you'll never know beyond your own lifetime, why worry about it? Enjoy the process. You'll be developing a philosophy of life and a philosophy of language. You won't have the time to worry about yourself, anyway.

I hope that this slender volume has given you one or two helpful thoughts or techniques. Let me share some last random thoughts.

Try to bear in mind that language is alive. It lives in millions of throats, it breathes with millions of lungs, and like the living organism it is, it grows. You've got to keep up with it.

Remember, too, that you have the right to make mistakes. Exercise it. Good judgment comes from experience, and often experience comes from bad judgment.

And lastly, a deadline is negative inspiration. Still, it's better than no inspiration at all.

I'll leave you with the Writer's Prayer.

I am one.
Let me become many.

# V

# A
# LITERARY
# CONSERVATORY

---

In order to become a surgeon, a person endures years of training, one cadaver, graduation, an internship with live (one hopes) patients, and finally, private practice. Becoming a skilled writer takes as many years as becoming a surgeon. However, there is no support for the process of becoming a writer. The emphasis is on the product. Writing can be taught. It is not a mysterious process. The basic and advanced principles of writing can be taught to anyone who demonstrates an aptitude for the work. True, there is genius, as there is in any field, but a competent individual can be turned into a fine craftsman, if not a blazing genius. Nowhere in the United States is there a program to train writers equivalent to medical school or that other worthy model, a music conservatory. There should be.

Language is the greatest resource of a culture. It is the repository of thought and the expression of dreams. No activity above the level of brute survival can be accomplished without language. When language is raised to the level of literature, one approaches heaven. Creating a program to develop writers is not a mere idyll for an English department. It is an act of cultural integrity.

What follows is an abbreviated model of a four-year program to form writers. What is not addressed here is aptitude tests and entrance requirements. This program starts at the point of student admission.

Each student is required to take Poetics 1A within the four-year span. Poets must complete all Poetics courses. They need not take the Technique courses with the exception of Technique 1A. All students must complete the Shakespeare series, outlined later, within their junior or senior years. So, poets take all the Poetics courses, which are rigorous training in all meters. Novelists, dramatists, and screenwriters must take all Technique courses. In the following breakdown, you will notice there are no nonfiction courses. Nonfiction is a journalistic instrument and not suitable for a true literary program.

FIRST YEAR, FIRST SEMESTER

Latin 1:          If a student has had four years of Latin s/he may choose an elective instead.

Anglo-Saxon

Reading:          Support materials attached regarding this requirement.

Poetics 1A:       All poets start here but this course must be completed by every student.

Technique 1A:     Must be taken by everyone. Technique 1A involves close study of the current English word pool. Anglo-Saxon and Latin 1 are a necessity for full understanding of word choice and implication.

Modern language of student's choice

FIRST YEAR, SECOND SEMESTER

Latin 1B

Reading

Poetics 1B:       Poets only.

Technique 1B:     All others. Focus on the difference between first person and third person in narrative.

Modern language 1B

Elective

SECOND YEAR, FIRST SEMESTER

Latin 2A

Reading

Poetics 2A:      Poets only.

Technique 2A:   All others. A careful examination of verbs, the constant tension between active voice and passive voice. Also, special emphasis will be centered on the lost subjunctive in English. By this time, each student will be struggling with the subjunctive in Latin.

Modern language 2A

Elective

SECOND YEAR, SECOND SEMESTER

Latin 2B

Reading

Poetics 2B:      Poets only.

Technique 2B:   All others. Students are now ready to consider the creation of character. Sex, race, and class must be considered here as well as idiosyncratic language. The author as hidden character must also be revealed, and this is sometimes quite a difficult topic.

Modern language 2B

Elective

THIRD YEAR, FIRST SEMESTER

Latin 3A

Reading

Poetics 3A:      Poets only.

Technique 3A:   All others. Advance character work. Field work is
                an exciting part of the advanced class. Students
                will be given specific character assignments.

Modern language 3A

Elective

THIRD YEAR, SECOND SEMESTER

Latin 3B

Reading

Poetics 3B:      Poets only.

Technique 3B:   All others. Students are now prepared for plot
                development. The basic plot lines will be studied.
                The effect of voice on plot will also be scrutinized.

Modern language 3B

Elective

FOURTH YEAR, FIRST SEMESTER

Latin 4A

Reading

Poetics 4A:      Poets only. If all meters have been mastered, this
                will be an independent study.

Technique 4A:   All others. Independent study. Student must be
                creating either a novel, a play, or a screenplay.

Modern language 4A

Elective

FOURTH YEAR, SECOND SEMESTER

Latin 4B

Reading

Poetics 4B:        Poets only. Independent study.

Technique 4B:    All others. Independent study.

Modern language 4B

Elective

REQUIRED SHAKESPEARE COURSE:

The plays of Shakespeare must be read and seen, if possible, in the order in which they were written. As BBC television has filmed the plays, it would be wonderful if the school had a library of those productions. It's much more important for a writer to see the plays then to read them. Shakespeare is perfect for students, since he combines all the disciplines within his work. This course will take two semesters. It is strongly suggested but not required that the student also take a history course of the Elizabethan Era, so s/he knows what Shakespeare's actual materials were.

ELECTIVES

Drama

Screenwriting

Publishing as an industry

Financial planning for writers

Nonfiction as a way to survive: This is not a true nonfiction course but rather a way to introduce students to markets that are not literary but which may help them support their literary work.

Greek and Roman literature

Literature courses from any non-English-speaking nation

Psychological survival for writers: Special attention will be given to substance abuse and to relationships with other people—people who are not creative.

It is hoped that some of these electives can be satisfied by the general college. It would not be within the scope of this program to hire people to teach, say, French literature.

The reading requirements are very simple: The student will read, in the order in which they were written, those works that are of permanent importance to the English language. Therefore the questions of style and content are paramount but only as the years go on. If you glance at the following reading list, you will see the early years are easy, since there is so little material. As publishing advances, more and more becomes available. I have culled what I think are the critical works but there is such a gargantuan body of literature written in the English language that my selections are bound to arouse debate. Also, I am weak in the areas of Australian, South African, and Canadian literature. While I have read authors of these nations, I just don't have a perspective on the body of national work. So, please forgive me if you are Australian, South African, or Canadian. I hope to correct my lack of depth here over the next five years.

I do repeat, these works must be read in the order in which they were written. Only in this manner can the student fully appreciate the growth and the majesty of the English language.

# VI

# AN
# ANNOTATED
# READING LIST

---

This list is prepared for you from a writer's point of view. Delightful though it is to read for story (and you will read for story) you have other concerns. You must study structure, evolving metaphor (if it exists within the work), style, originality, and boldness of theme. Does the dialogue work? Are the characters real or are they stick figures manipulated to serve the story? Is the voice an honest voice or is the author hiding something from you? (Hiding something is not necessarily negative; it may serve the story.) Does the author trust the reader/audience? Has ego gotten in the way of the work itself? Does the work hark back to earlier works by other writers?

There are many more questions than these, but as you can see, your concerns are both emotional and technical. This is what makes our work so subjective.

In the beginning of this list you will be absorbing our language in its primitive state. You begin your reading in the seventh century A.D. As you read, keep in mind that other languages (Greek and Latin for Western culture) have reached their full genius. Look at where we started. The language is stark, not fluid. The concern of the author is usually to inform you of an historical event. *Beowulf* is the first work to reveal the raw visual power of Anglo-Saxon.

These early works—and I've picked out only a few—serve to

ground you in your language and in some of the consistent themes
of our culture/language. As the centuries progress, so does the
language. Chaucer, at the end of the fourteenth century, brought
forth the revolution. You and I are indebted to him. He raised up
the language. He understood the peculiar affinity of our language/
people for comedy/comic relief.

After Chaucer, improvements are rapid. You will be amazed at
just how quickly the language evolved. English writers took advantage of each improvement. Nor did they mind stealing from one
another or plundering writers from other times and nations.

Writing was, and essentially remains, an aristocratic pursuit.
In order to get the time to write you must be an aristocrat or be
sponsored by one. Today, sponsorship has been taken over by your
publisher. But writing is a time-consuming occupation. Your literary ancestors, recognizing the need for patronage, wrote about
kings, queens, dukes, and duchesses. Naturally, a flattering reference to one's own patron is found within the work. Don't be put off
by this "class" concern. The common people found their outlet in
plays. Since they couldn't read and write, plays were extremely
important to them not just as entertainment but as education. So
as you move through this list you will see the difference between
what was written to be read and what was written to be performed.
Keep this uppermost in your mind or you will miss the point the
author was trying to make.

Reading these works in chronological order will begin to
reveal you to you. You will find that you have predecessors. Even
though you may feel isolated historically, you are not. Somewhere
in this reading list is a writer or writers with whom you have a
natural affinity. When you find them, cherish them. They will teach
you a lot.

Another fact that may be revealed to you is your own attention
span. If you are under forty-five you have probably always known
television. (I did not. We were poor and I didn't see a television
until I was about seven). The misery of television is commercials.
On the average, you watch for twelve and a half minutes and then

the show cuts to a commercial. Today, our attention span is shorter than that of even one generation ahead of us. If you find yourself getting fidgety or bored, ask yourself if it's the material or if it's you. Granted, some of the selections contained here are boring but you must address them. Still, people under forty-five have been damaged in terms of their attention span. They also need action in the plot. I don't know if people can be weaned away from this need for hype or a fix. I cannot single-handedly change our collective attention spans. All I can do is alert you to something that's happened to you as a result of circumstance. This is a dangerous development for writers, because some subjects can only be approached slowly. I think of them as sleeping cobras. If the public has to have action and false drama (i.e., melodrama), then the more upsetting issues of human life are going to lie dormant because we won't have the patience to understand them.

If that paragraph isn't clear now, it will be as you go through this list. When you come upon the late eighteenth and nineteenth centuries you will see that novels were expected to consume your time. Readers had tolerance for embellishments, the exploration of tangents to the plot, and so on. Of course, they didn't have film and television to distract them. There were no professional sports as we understand them, although there were sports. Reading was a primary form of entertainment and writers rose to the occasion. You do not have that pride of place.

Originally, this list was much more complete. My publisher beseeched me to cut it down to the bone because it would take up too much space and raise the price of the book. I apologize for many of the important works left out. If you would like the complete list, which is especially useful for the early centuries of our literature, turn to the back of the book for more information.

In some instances I have assumed you have read what is considered a writer's masterpiece. Often I have included a writer's first work so you could see the beginnings of talent. If the writer is important I have included later works too. I have also included some failures and some popular novels. You need the comparison.

You can't understand what is good until you know what is mediocre or bad. I find that often the most interesting works from the past are the ones in which the author had an original idea and couldn't fulfill it.

Another thing: Try to cleanse your mind of what your English teachers told you. They were reading with a different purpose from yours. They were also confining themselves to what has been generally accepted as high-quality literature. High quality, depending on where and when you went to school, can mean sterile and sanitized. Beware. You can't afford to think in terms of good and bad right now. You must think in terms of what works and what doesn't. Once you are secure about the mechanics of literature, you can apply yourself to the aesthetics of literature.

After this reading list, which is restricted to writers of English, I wish I could make one from all Western literature, but there just isn't room.

I wish we were gathered among other working writers to read together. Each person brings something unique to a work of literature and I will miss the discussions we aren't having. However, I do hope this helps you and that you'll stick with it over the years.

# READING LIST

The dates below are dates of publication, or public showing in the case of plays. They do not correspond with the dates of authorship.

### 665–670
Caedmon, *Caedmon's Hymn,* recorded in the Venerable Bede's *Ecclesiastical History of the English People.*

### ca. 700
Anonymous, *Beowulf.*

### 700–800
Anonymous, *The Rhyming Poem.*

### 780–830
Cynewulf (attrib.), *Andreas; Christ; Elene; The Fates of the Apostles; Juliana; Riddles* 1–59, 30b, 60–95; *The Dream of the Rood.* Pick one of Cynewulf's works.

### 856–915
Anonymous, *Judith.* Begins the written tradition, as the influence of Cynewulf can be clearly seen in this poet's work.

Bede, Venerabilis. *An Ecclesiastical History of the English People.*

### 973
Anonymous, *The Coronation of Edgar,* in *The Anglo-Saxon Chroni-*

*cle.* The poet-monk's rhapsodizing on the fact that the apocalypse was only twenty-seven years away is entertaining, and more interesting than the story of Edgar's coronation.

### 975
Anonymous, *The Death of Edgar,* in *The Anglo-Saxon Chronicle.*

### ca. 800–1000
Anonymous, *The Banished Wife's Complaint.*

Anonymous, *A Love Letter.*

Anonymous, *The Ruined City.*

### ca. 1300
Anonymous, *Piers Plowman.* First extant copy dates from 1360, but it is mentioned before then.

### ca. 1350–1400
John Barbour, *The Actes and Life of the Most Victorious Conqueror, Robert Bruce, King of Scotland.* First extant copy, 1487.

Geoffrey Chaucer, If you haven't read *The Canterbury Tales,* do. It's a delight. If you have, then pick another of Chaucer's work.

### ca. 1394-1395
Sir Thomas Clanvowe, *The Cuckoo and the Nightingale.*

### ca. 1400
"The Pearl Poet," *Sir Gawaine and the Grene Knight.*

### 1423
James I, King of Scotland, *The Kingis Quair.*

### 1470
Sir Thomas Malory, *Le Morte d'Arthur.*

### 1481
Anonymous, *Reynard the Fox.*

### 1483
John Gower, *Confessio Amantis.*

## 1528

John Skelton, *A Replication Against Certain Young Scholars*. The language is antiquated but the ideas are current.

## 1533

John Heywood, *The Play of the Weather*.

## 1545

John Skelton, *Why Come Ye Not to Court?*

## 1551

Sir Thomas More, *Utopia* (first edition in English, translated by Ralph Robinson).

## 1566

Nicholas Udall, *Ralph Roister Doister*. This will give you an idea of how humor was used, and it will also show you how different Shakespeare was from his contemporaries. The play smacks of the schoolroom.

## 1581

Barnabe Rich, *His Farewell to the Militarie Profession*.

## 1583

Robert Greene, *Mamillia, A Mirrour o Looking-Glasse for the Ladies of England*.

## 1590

Robert Greene, *Greenes Never Too Late*.

Christopher Marlowe, *Tamburlaine the Great, Divided into Two Tragical Discourses*.

## 1591

Thomas Lodge, *A Margarite of America*.

Sir Philip Sidney, *Astrophel and Stella*.

Edmund Spenser, *Complaints, Containing Sundry Small Poems of the World's Vanity*.

### 1593

William Shakespeare, *Venus and Adonis.*

### 1594

First production of Shakespeare's *Comedy of Errors.* You should buy a *Complete Works of Shakespeare* and read it in chronological order. There's no way around this, and in addition, once you get the hang of the language you will be swept into its beauty.

Christopher Marlowe, *Edward the Second.*

### 1596

Michael Drayton, *The Tragical Legend of Robert, Duke of Normandy; The Legend of Matilda; The Legend of Piers Gaveston.*

### 1598

John Dickenson, *Greene in Conceipt: New Raised from His Grave to the Tragique Historie of the Fair Valeria of London.*

John Marston, *The Metamorphosis of Pigmalions Image, and Certaine Satyres,* and *The Scourge of Villainy: Three Books of Satyres.*

### 1600

Ben Jonson, *Every Man Out of His Humour.* See also *Complete Poems,* edited by Ian Donaldson, 1975.

Thomas Nashe, *Summer's Last Will and Testament.*

### 1601

Ben Jonson, *Every Man in His Humour.*

### 1603

Thomas Dekker, *The Wonderful Yeare, Wherein Is Shown the Picture of London Lying Sick of the Plague.*

### 1604

Christopher Marlowe, *The Tragicall History of D. Faustus.*

Thomas Middleton (with Thomas Dekker), *The Honest Whore.*

### 1606

John Marston, *The Wonder of Women, or The Tragedy of Sophonisba.*

### 1607

Ben Jonson, *Volpone, or The Fox*.

George Peele, *The Merrie Conceited Jests of George Peele*.

### 1608

François de Belleforest, *The History of Hamblet*.

Thomas Middleton, *A Mad World, My Masters*.

### 1609

Edmund Spenser, *The Faerie Queene, Disposed into Twelve Books, Fashioning XII Moral Virtues*, with *Mutability Cantos*. *The Faerie Queene* was originally published 1590–96, without the *Mutability Cantos*.

### 1611

John Donne, *An Anatomy of the World*.

### 1612

Ben Jonson, *The Alchemist*.

### 1613

Francis Beaumont, *The Knight of the Burning Pestle*.

### 1620

Thomas Middleton, and William Rowley, *The World Tost at Tennis*.

### 1633

John Donne, *Poems*.

Christopher Marlowe, *The Famous Tragedy of the Rich Jew of Malta*.

### 1641

John Day, *The Parliament of Bees, with Their Proper Characters*.

### 1650

Anne Bradstreet, *The Tenth Muse Lately Sprung Up in America*. Anne Bradstreet strikes a blow for women writers.

## 1653

Izaak Walton, *The Compleat Angler*. A gentle, enjoyable book even if you don't like fishing.

## 1656

Margaret Cavendish, Duchess of Newcastle, *Nature's Pictures Drawn by Fancies Pencil to the Life*. The Duchess of Newcastle fancies too much.

## 1658

Sidney Godolphin, *The Passion of Dido for Aeneas*. "Sidney Godolphin is an almost perfect example of a truly minor poet ... of the nearly 1,000 lines of his original verse, not one is memorably bad; nor is there a single line that is memorably good"—THOMAS WHEELER. (Couldn't resist.)

## 1667

John Milton, *Paradise Lost*. I don't like Milton, even as I recognize his exalted gift for poetry. Still, he must be read and he must be mastered.

## 1669

John Dryden, *Tyrannic Love, or The Royal Martyr*.

## 1671

Bryce Blair, *The Vision of Theodorus Verax*. This gives you a sense of Milton's contemporaries.

John Milton, *Paradise Regained, to Which Is Added Samson Agonistes*.

## 1673

John Dryden, *Marriage A-la-Mode*.

William Wycherley, *The Gentleman Dancing-Master*. Wycherley is working out the "new" comedy of manners for English speakers.

## 1675

William Wycherley, *The Country Wife*.

## 1677

William Wycherley, *The Plain Dealer*.

## 1678

John Bunyan, *The Pilgrim's Progress from This World to That Which Is to Come*.

John Dryden, *All for Love, or The World Well Lost*, and *MacFlecknoe*.

## 1679

Andrew Marvell, *Advice to a Painter*. See also Marvell's *Complete Poems*, edited by Elizabeth Story Donno, 1972.

## 1680

Thomas D'Urfey, *The Virtuous Wife, or Good Luck at Last*.

## 1684

Aphra Behn, *The Adventures of the Black Lady*.

## 1686

Aphra Behn, *The Lover's Watch*.

## 1688

Richard Blackbourn, *Wit in a Woman*.

## 1689

Nathaniel Lee, *The Princess of Cleve*.

## 1692

William Congreve, *Incognita, or Love and Duty Reconciled*. Congreve takes on Wycherley, in a sense. He is good and he's going to get better.

## 1693

William Congreve, *The Old Bachelor*.

## 1695

William Congreve, *Love for Love*.

## 1697

William Congreve, *The Mourning Bride*.

## 1698

John Crowne, *Calisto*. I threw this in by way of contrast. Crowne is not especially gifted but he's trying.

## 1699

William King, *Dialogues of the Dead.*

## 1700

William Congreve, *The Way of the World*. You can't get much better than this. Restoration drama in its exalted state.

## 1701

Nicholas Rowe, *Tamerlane*. Precedes Arnold Schwartzenegger by 286 years! Rowe would have made him Tamerlane.

## 1704

Jonathan Swift, *A Tale of a Tub, Written for the Universal Improvement of Mankind, to Which Is Added an Account of a Battle Between the Ancient and Modern Books in St. James's Library.* The first appearance of this satiric genius.

## 1707

George Farquhar, *The Beaux' Stratagem*. Farquhar lacks Congreve's and Sheridan's natural talent but he works hard; he pays attention to structure although this may be difficult for a modern reader to realize. This is a very fine piece of work.

## 1708

Ebenezer Cooke, *The Sot-Weed Factor, or A Voyage to Maryland.*

## 1709

Susanna Centlivre, *The Busie Body, A Comedy*. Susanna makes a stab at it.

## 1714

Alexander Pope, *The Rape of the Lock*. Divine artifice. Even if an author could achieve this in our time, our public is not sophisticated enough to enjoy it. (I hope I'm wrong.)

## 1715

Susanna Centlivre, *The Gotham Election*. Never acted, due to censorship. Susanna has not given up, but she's in trouble.

## 1719

Daniel Defoe, *The Life and Strange Surprising Adventures of Robinson Crusoe, of York, Mariner*. Here's a "newspaperman" turned author.

## 1726

Jonathan Swift, *Travels into Several Remote Nations of the World, by Captain Lemuel Gulliver*. What can I say that has not already been said? Swift is savage and very secure in his style.

## 1734

Jonathan Swift, *A Beautiful Young Nymph Going to Bed*.

## 1737

Elizabeth Boyd, *The Happy Unfortunate; or The Female Page*. An old theme.

## 1739

Jonathan Swift, *Verses on the Death of Dr. Swift*. Swift's mind is beginning to go.

## 1740

Samuel Richardson, *Pamela, or Virtue Rewarded*. You can argue about whether or not this is the first true novel. I think the *Satyricon* is the first real novel in Western literature and I know I'll get an argument there. But sticking to English, this has importance and we all need to read it at least once.

## 1743

John Gay, *The Distress'd Wife*.

## 1747

Thomas Gray, *Ode on a Distant Prospect of Eton College*. Early Gray.

### 1749
Henry Fielding, *The History of Tom Jones, a Foundling*.

Samuel Johnson, *The Vanity of Human Wishes: The Tenth Satire of Juvenal Imitated*.

### 1751
Thomas Gray, *An Elegy Wrote in a Country Church Yard*. Gray in best voice.

### 1756
Christopher Smart, *On the Goodness of the Supreme Being*. "Confinement in the madhouse allowed Smart to escape some of the restrictions of demand and tradition, and create the distinctive religious verse which is his main achievement"— MARCUS WALSH.

### 1757
Thomas Gray, *Odes*.

### 1762
James Macpherson, *Fingal: An Ancient Epic, with Several Other Poems Translated from the Gaelic Language*. Macpherson's claim that these poems are the work of an ancient Gaelic Makar named Ossian is fantasy. They are his own work.

Tobias Smollett, *The Adventures of Sir Launcelot Greaves*.

### 1766
Oliver Goldsmith, *The Vicar of Wakefield*. Another giant steps on the scene.

### 1768
Oliver Goldsmith, *The Good Natur'd Man*.

Thomas Gray, *Poems*.

Lady Mary Wortley Montagu, *Poetical Works*.

### 1769
Tobias Smollett, *The History and Adventures of an Atom*.

## 1770

Oliver Goldsmith, *The Deserted Village.*

Phyllis Wheatley, *An Elegiac Poem on the Death of the Celebrated Divine Georg Whitfield.*

## 1773

Oliver Goldsmith, *She Stoops to Conquer, or The Mistakes of a Night.* Sheer, audacious fun!

## 1775

Richard Brinsley Sheridan, *The Duenna* (music by Thomas Linley). A respectable beginning for another magical writer.

## 1777

William Combe, *The Diaboliad. A Poem. Dedicated to the Worst Man in His Majesty's Dominions,* Vol. 1. The concept is better than the execution.

## 1780

Richard Brinsley Sheridan, *The School for Scandal.* How lucky were our forebears that they lived at the same time as Goldsmith and Sheridan. Our theater, today, doesn't even come close.

## 1781

Richard Brinsley Sheridan, *The Critic, or A Tragedy Rehearsed.*

## 1785

James Boswell, *The Journal of a Tour to the Hebrides with Samuel Johnson.* Welcome to modern biography, the first bud.

## 1789

William Blake, *Songs of Innocence.*

## 1791

James Boswell, *The Life of Samuel Johnson,* 2 Vols. The full bloom.

## 1796

Joel Barlow, *The Hasty Pudding.*

Samuel Taylor Coleridge, *Poems on Various Subjects.*

Thomas Morton, *The Way to Get Married.* It isn't great literature but it's interesting to note that this subject is still addressed today.

### 1798
Samuel Taylor Coleridge, and William Wordsworth, *Lyrical Ballads, with a Few Other Poems.*

William Cowper, *Poems: On the Receipt of My Mother's Picture; The Dog and Waterlily.*

### 1810
Marjorie Fleming. A child poet writing 1810–1811. A literary curiosity worth looking into. Accessible in various collections and referred to sporadically by Victorian writers. Her *Complete Works* is available at most closed-stack research libraries.

Sir Walter Scott, *The Lady of the Lake.* This man eventually became an industry. The story line of each of his novels is strong. The tone is unabashed romanticism.

### 1813
Jane Austen, *Pride and Prejudice.*

### 1814
Fanny Burney, *The Wanderer, or Female Difficulties.*

### 1816
Samuel Taylor Coleridge, *Christabel; Kubla Khan: A Vision; The Poems of Sleep.*

Percy Bysshe Shelley, *Alastor, or The Spirit of Solitude, and Other Poems.* It's interesting to contrast Keats with Shelley. I'll let you make your own judgment.

### 1817
John Keats, *Poems.*

Sir Walter Scott, *Rob Roy.*

## 1818

Jane Austen, *Northanger Abbey* and *Persuasion.* See also *Love and Friendship,* edited by G. K. Chesterton, 1922; *The Watsons,* edited by A. B. Walkley, 1923; *Lady Susan,* edited by Q. D. Davis, 1958.

Hannah More, *Stories for the Middle Ranks of Society* and *Tales for the Common People.*

Sir Walter Scott, *The Heart of Midlothian.*

Mary Wollstonecraft Shelley, *Frankenstein, or The Modern Prometheus.*

## 1819

Sir Walter Scott, *Ivanhoe: A Romance.*

## 1820

Washington Irving, *The Sketch Book of Geoffrey Crayon, Gent.,* 2 Vols. The first American author to attain international fame. He is much better than we give him credit for being. Literature has fashions and right now Irving is out of fashion.

Percy Bysshe Shelley, *Prometheus Unbound: A Lyrical Drama with Other Poems.*

## 1821

James Fenimore Cooper, *The Spy.*

Sir Walter Scott, *Kenilworth: A Romance.*

## 1824

Washington Irving, *Tales of a Traveller.* Irving is getting better.

Walter Savage Landor, *Imaginary Conversations of Literary Men and Statesmen,* 5 Vols. I find this work rewarding to read.

## 1825

Sarah Kemble Knight, *The Journal of Sarah Kemble Knight.* Sarah learned the secrets of self-advertisement.

## 1826

James Fenimore Cooper, *The Last of the Mohicans*. His dark vision, almost devoid of women, remains intact. It would have been impossible for a European to write this novel.

## 1827

Edgar Allan Poe, *Tamerlane and Other Poems*.

## 1831

James Fenimore Cooper, *The Water Witch*. It's a good idea to read one of his novels that isn't his best. Gives us all hope.

Edgar Allan Poe, *Poems*.

## 1832

Washington Irving, *The Alhambra*. I think this is an underrated book. It's travel writing of the highest order.

## 1837

Charles Dickens, *The Posthumous Papers of the Pickwick Club*. Even from the first, Dickens was different.

Nathaniel Hawthorne, *Twice-Told Tales*.

## 1838

Elizabeth Barrett Browning, *The Seraphim and Other Poems*.

## 1840

James Fenimore Cooper, *The Pathfinder*. Pure Cooper. Pure homoerotic myth-making, I think!

Edgar Allan Poe, *Tales of the Grotesque and Arabesque*.

## 1841

James Fenimore Cooper, *The Deerslayer*. Even better than *The Pathfinder*.

## 1843

Edgar Allan Poe, *The Murders in the Rue Morgue* and *The Man*

*That Was Used Up.* Poe was clever, original and completely misunderstood.

### 1845

Edgar Allan Poe, *Tales* and *The Raven and Other Poems.*

### 1847

Anne Brontë, *Agnes Grey.*

Charlotte Brontë, *Jane Eyre: An Autobiography.* See how background and family impose upon literature.

Emily Brontë, *Wuthering Heights.* See also her *Complete Poems,* edited by C. W. Hatfield, 1941.

### 1848

James Russell Lowell, *A Fable for Critics.* A "civilized" voice for the Northeast.

William Makepeace Thackeray, *Vanity Fair: A Novel Without a Hero.* Not true. The hero was the author.

### 1849

Robert Browning, *Poems,* 2 Vols.

James Russell Lowell, *Poems,* 2 Vols.

### 1850

Nathaniel Hawthorne, *The Scarlet Letter.*

Alfred, Lord Tennyson, *In Memoriam.* Tennyson's voice is elegant. If you've been reading your poetry, you will "hear" the difference instantly.

### 1851

Nathaniel Hawthorne, *The House of the Seven Gables* and *The Snow Image and Other Twice-Told Tales.*

Herman Melville, *Moby Dick, Or The White Whale.* More homoerotic, desperate literature. There is a doom-ridden quality to Melville and Cooper that astonishes me.

George Meredith, *Poems*. Technically, Meredith is superb, but I still find him boring.

## 1852

Harriet Beecher Stowe, *Uncle Tom's Cabin, or Life Among the Lowly*. You have to read it to grasp how bad it really is and to wonder at its tremendous political impact.

## 1853

Walter Savage Landor, *Imaginary Conversations of Greeks and Romans*. More joy.

## 1854

George Washington Harris, *Sut Lovingood's Yarns and High Times and Hard Times*. Serialized, beginning November 4, 1854, in *Spirit of the Times* magazine; first published in 1966–1967, 2 vols., with M. Thomas Inge as editor. Harris gets "cute" but it's a minor school of writing still in vogue today, usually among columnists and magazine writers. The style is updated, obviously, but you will recognize the tone and possibly be nauseated.

Henry David Thoreau, *Walden, or Life in the Woods*. Overrated and overindulged. One has to read him to try to grasp the phenomenon, particularly as it affected Americans in the late 1960's.

## 1855

Henry Wadsworth Longfellow, *The Song of Hiawatha*. He's better than you think.

Walt Whitman, *Leaves of Grass*.

## 1857

Herman Melville, *The Confidence-Man: His Masquerade*. You should read a novel that wasn't a big success. Each of us needs to be reminded that famous, dead writers struggled as much as we struggle.

## 1858

Oliver Wendell Holmes, *The Autocrat of the Breakfast Table*.

## 1862

George Meredith, *Modern Love*. Extremely interesting, especially when compared to his other poems.

## 1865

Lewis Carroll, *Alice's Adventures in Wonderland*.

## 1866

Christina Rossetti, *The Prince's Progress and Other Poems*.

Algernon Charles Swinburne, *Poems and Ballads*.

## 1867

Samuel L. Clemens (Mark Twain, *The Celebrated Jumping Frog of Calaveras County and Other Sketches*.

Ouida (pseudonym for Marie Louise de la Rámee), *Under Two Flags*. A wonderful example of a "popular" novel.

## 1868

Louisa May Alcott, *Little Women*, Vol. 1. True Americana.

Walt Whitman, *Poems*.

## 1869

Louisa May Alcott, *Little Women*, Vol. 2. More of the same.

Samuel L. Clemens, *The Innocents Abroad*. Conceptually, this was a big jump (forgive the pun) from *The Celebrated Frog*. . . .

Henry Kendall, *Leaves from Australian Forests*. At last, something about Australia.

## 1870

Edward Lear, *Nonsense Songs, Stories, Botany, and Alphabets*.

Dante Gabriel Rossetti, *Poems*.

## 1872

Samuel Butler, *Erewhon, or Over the Range*. There are other Butlers, but this clearly demonstrates his themes.

George Eliot, *Middlemarch: A Study of Provincial Life.* This was a trial to read in eleventh grade but from a technical viewpoint it is a successful novel.

### 1873
Ambrose Bierce, *Nuggets and Dust Panned Out in California.* If you get "hooked" on him, you'll read everything he wrote.

### 1874
Thomas Hardy, *Far from the Madding Crowd.*

### 1875
William Cullen Bryant, *Poems,* 3 Vols.

### 1876
Samuel L. Clemens, *The Adventures of Tom Sawyer.*

Henry Wheeler Shaw, *Josh Billings, His Works Complete.*

### 1877
Sidney Lanier, *Poems.*

### 1878
W. S. Gilbert, *H.M.S. Pinafore* (music by Arthur Sullivan). How did Gilbert learn to be Gilbert? Where is he now that we need him? Don't mistake him for just a lyricist.

### 1879
W. S. Gilbert, *The Pirates of Penzance* (music by Arthur Sullivan).

Bret Harte, *An Heiress of Red Dog and Other Sketches.*

George Meredith, *The Egoist.* The concern of "Modern Love" is now disguised as a novel which is almost a comedy of manners. I believe it is the same idea from a new angle. Meredith appeals to intellectuals. In my mind, T. S. Eliot picks up where Meredith left off.

### 1881
Joel Chandler Harris, *Uncle Remus, His Songs and His Sayings.*

Still remarkable, although you must steel yourself for the "cute" racism.

Oscar Wilde, *Poems.*

## 1883
Samuel L. Clemens, *Life on the Mississippi.* He's learned a great deal about writing. It shows.

Robert Louis Stevenson, *Treasure Island.* He's much better than a popular novelist, yet rarely is he regarded as "literary." Make up your own mind.

## 1885
Samuel L. Clemens, *The Adventures of Huckleberry Finn.*

Walter Pater, *Marius the Epicurean: His Sensations and Ideas.*

## 1886
Robert Louis Stevenson, *The Strange Case of Dr. Jekyll and Mr. Hyde.* Much, much more than a horror "movie." This work is thematically brilliant.

## 1888
Edward Bellamy, *Looking Backward: 2000–1887.*

Rudyard Kipling, *Plain Tales from the Hills.* Rivers will flow from this pen.

## 1890
James Whitcomb Riley, *Rhymes of Childhood.*

## 1891
Oscar Wilde, *The Picture of Dorian Gray.* Close, in a thematic sense, to *Dr. Jekyll and Mr. Hyde,* yet filled with cynicism. Wilde is always stylized. Stevenson is more "natural."

## 1892
Sir Arthur Conan Doyle, *The Adventures of Sherlock Holmes.* Elementary.

W. S. Gilbert, *Rosencrantz and Guildenstern.*

### 1893
Samuel L. Clemens, *The £1,000,000 Bank Note.* Mark Twain off-form is as interesting as other writers on-form.

Oscar Wilde, *Lady Windermere's Fan: A Play About a Good Woman.*

### 1895
Stephen Crane, *The Black Riders and Other Lines.* You've already read *The Red Badge of Courage.*

Sir Arthur Wing Pinero, *The Second Mrs. Tanqueray.*

H. G. Wells, *The Time Machine: An Invention.* He was never anything like any other writer. A true original, although not "great."

### 1896
Samuel L. Clemens, *Personal Recollections of Joan of Arc.*

### 1897
Kate Chopin, *A Night in Acadie.* Kate Chopin did a brisk sale in books and she wrote many. She is very much a product of her time.

Bram Stoker, *Dracula.*

### 1898
George Bernard Shaw, *Plays Pleasant and Unpleasant,* 2 Vols. He asked for no quarter and he gave none, from youth to old age.

H. G. Wells, *The War of the Worlds.*

Oscar Wilde, *The Ballad of Reading Gaol.* This was a shift for Wilde.

### 1900
L. Frank Baum, *The Wonderful Wizard of Oz.* See what happens when a work is adapted for the screen.

Joseph Conrad, *Lord Jim*. Pay attention to how a non-native uses English.

Theodore Dreiser, *Sister Carrie*.

### 1901
George Washington Cable, *The Cavalier*. Cable was much admired in his day. He filled the shelves of book stores.

Frank Norris, *The Octopus*. This floored people.

### 1903
Samuel Butler, *The Way of All Flesh*.

George Bernard Shaw, *Man and Superman: A Comedy (and a Philosophy)*.

### 1904
O. Henry (pseudonym of William Sydney Porter), *Cabbages and Kings*. Fantastic command over the short-story form.

### 1905
Edith Wharton, *The House of Mirth*. This is a sharp, new American voice. In my mind she is the counterpoint to Dreiser.

### 1906
Upton Sinclair, *The Jungle*. What did he learn from Frank Norris? Do you think there is a connection?

### 1907
J. M. Synge, *The Playboy of the Western World*.

### 1908
Kenneth Grahame, *The Wind in the Willows*. Utter happiness/ silliness.

### 1909
Samuel L. Clemens, *Extracts from Captain Stormfield's Visit to Heaven*.

Gertrude Stein, *Three Lives: Stories of The Good Anna, Melanctha, and The Gentle Lena.* She is rough going but her experiments with language helped her generation of writers break from the adjective-heavy style then so popular. If Hemingway had not found Stein, he would not have become Hemingway.

### 1910

Saki (pseudonym of H. H. Munro), *Reginald in Russia and Other Sketches.*

William Butler Yeats, *The Green Helmet and Other Poems.* He is to poetry as Cezanne is to painting.

### 1911

Max Beerbohm, *Zuleika Dobson, or An Oxford Love Story.*

Frances Hodgson Burnett, *The Secret Garden.*

Edith Wharton, *Ethan Frome.* Remember reading this in high school? Bet it looks different now.

### 1912

Zane Grey, *Riders of the Purple Sage.* These cowboy stories were gobbled up by little boys in America and also in Germany.

### 1913

D. H. Lawrence, *Sons and Lovers.* More interesting than *Lady Chatterley's Lover.*

Vachel Lindsay, *General William Booth Enters into Heaven and Other Poems.*

### 1914

Edgar Rice Burroughs, *Tarzan of the Apes.* Another one of those boys' books which affected so many people.

Booth Tarkington, *Penrod.* Tarkington, for a time, was a beloved American writer. Read this and see if you can figure out why he is out of favor. Almost forgotten.

## 1915

Edgar Lee Masters, *Spoon River Anthology* (revised and expanded in 1916). This is a deceptive work.

## 1916

Samuel L. Clemens, *The Mysterious Stranger.*

George Bernard Shaw, *Pygmalion; Overruled;* and *Androcles and the Lion.*

## 1917

Clemence Dane, *Regiment of Women.* She was very celebrated in her time.

Siegfried Sassoon, *To Any Dead Officer.* He is not a great or perhaps even good writer by literary standards, but he is effective and his reserve is probably what cost him greatness, for the talent is there. Also, he did not devote himself to the craft.

## 1918

Gerard Manley Hopkins (d. 1889), *Poems,* edited by Robert Bridges.

Booth Tarkington, *The Magnificent Ambersons.* This book should not be in the literary doldrums.

## 1919

P. G. Wodehouse, *My Man Jeeves.* The beginning of an industry much more appreciated by the British than by Americans.

## 1920

Dame Agatha Christie, *The Mysterious Affair at Styles.* Doyle's spiritual "daughter" begins to weave her web.

Wilfred Owen (d. 1918), *Poems,* edited by Siegfried Sassoon. See also *Collected Poems,* edited by C. Day Lewis.

Edith Wharton, *The Age of Innocence.* A devastating book—and it fools you. She has become so sure of herself she doesn't have to show off.

## 1921

Clemence Dane, *Will Shakespeare: An Invention in Four Acts.* What do you think is going on here? Is this clever or is there something else?

## 1922

T. S. Eliot, *The Waste Land.* The post-World War I world found a voice.

John Galsworthy, *The Forsyte Saga.*

James Joyce, *Ulysses.* Where would university professors be without *Ulysses*? By this time, this work has become a parody of itself and it is the fawning of university English teachers that has ruined it. What a pity.

Katherine Mansfield, *The Garden Party and Other Stories.*

## 1923

Edna St. Vincent Millay, *Poems.* A crystal clear, unyielding voice.

## 1924

Emily Dickinson (d. 1886), *The Complete Poems,* edited by Martha Dickinson Bianchi.

Edna Ferber, *So Big.* Her sense of story is sure. You may or may not find her "dated." She enjoyed stupendous success in her lifetime.

George Bernard Shaw, *Saint Joan.*

## 1925

Noel Coward, *The Vortex.* Daring at the time. Coward's subject was VD.

Countee Cullen, *Color.*

Hilda Doolittle (H.D.), *Collected Poems.*

Theodore Dreiser, *An American Tragedy.*

F. Scott Fitzgerald, *The Great Gatsby.*

Robinson Jeffers, *Roan Stallion, Tamar, and Other Poems.*

Sinclair Lewis, *Arrowsmith.*

### 1926

Ernest Hemingway, *The Sun Also Rises.* I never tire of this novel.

Sean O'Casey, *The Plough and the Stars.*

Sir Sacheverell Sitwell, *All Summer in a Day: An Autobiographical Fantasia.* You may hate it or love it. This is what happens when a writer is "superior" to his audience. Very different from his sister, Edith.

### 1927

Rosamond Lehmann, *Dusty Answer.*

Jean Rhys, *The Left Bank and Other Stories.*

Thornton Wilder, *The Bridge of San Luis Rey.*

Virginia Woolf, *To the Lighthouse.*

### 1928

J. M. Barrie, *Peter Pan, or The Boy Who Would Not Grow Up.*

Radclyffe Hall, *The Well of Loneliness.* Historically important as regards women. Stylistically absurd.

D. H. Lawrence, *Lady Chatterley's Lover.* Another historically important work of questionable literary value. As time passes the cracks in the plaster widen, and Lawrence fanatics will blow a fuse when they read this assessment.

Virginia Woolf, *Orlando: A Biography.* I believe this is her greatest work. I know I'll get lots of arguments but that's why Woolf is special. She involves you in her work in a personal way.

### 1929

Djuna Barnes, *A Night Among the Horses.*

Dashiell Hammett, *The Dain Curse.*

Edmund Wilson, *I Thought of Daisy.*

Thomas Wolfe, *Look Homeward Angel: A Story of the Buried Life.*

## 1930

Dorothy Canfield (later Fisher), *The Deepening Stream.* She was very popular.

Noel Coward, *Private Lives.* Bliss. Pure bliss.

W. Somerset Maugham, *Cakes and Ale.* His is a "distant" style. Very readable. He is tricky but you don't know you are being tricked—or maybe it's just me.

Carl Van Vechten, *Parties: Scenes from Contemporary New York Life.*

## 1931

Elizabeth Bowen, *Friends and Relations.*

Kay Boyle, *Plagued by the Nightingale.*

Pearl S. Buck, *The Good Earth.* Another writer in eclipse.

Gertrude Stein, *How to Write.* Dare we try after reading this?

## 1932

Erskine Caldwell, *Tobacco Road.* Certain Southerners were very upset with Caldwell. He didn't flinch.

William Faulkner, *Light in August.* Another Southerner despised, in the beginning, by his own people. He didn't give up either.

Zelda Fitzgerald, *Save Me the Waltz.*

Rosamond Lehmann, *Invitation to the Waltz.*

James Thurber, *The Seal in the Bedroom and Other Predicaments.*

## 1933

Richard Aldington, *All Men are Enemies: A Romance.* Another popular novelist.

Ivy Compton-Burnett, *More Women Than Men.* She was much praised back then.

Dorothy L. Sayers, *Murder Must Advertise.*

Gertrude Stein, *The Autobiography of Alice B. Toklas.* At last, you can understand what she's writing.

Nathanael West, *Miss Lonelyhearts.*

## 1934

Robert Graves, *I, Claudius* and *Claudius the God.*

Dashiell Hammett, *The Thin Man.*

Lillian Hellman, *The Children's Hour.*

Zora Neale Hurston, *Jonah's Gourd Vine.*

Frederick Rolfe (pseudonym of Baron Corvo), *The Desire and Pursuit of the Whole.* A curiosity then. A curiosity still.

## 1935

T. S. Eliot, *Murder in the Cathedral.* If only he hadn't been so intellectual!

Hugh MacDiarmid, *Second Hymn to Lenin and Other Poems.*

John O'Hara, *Butterfield 8.* A smashing success. Most of his books were best sellers. Can you figure out why?

Muriel Rukeyser, *Theory of Flight.*

## 1936

Djuna Barnes, *Nightwood.* This is considered her strange, isolated masterpiece.

Margaret Mitchell, *Gone with the Wind.* Don't laugh. If you pay attention to this novel you might learn something.

Dorothy Parker, *Collected Poems: Not So Deep as a Well.*

Laura Riding, *Progress of Stories.*

### 1937
Moss Hart and George S. Kaufman, *You Can't Take It with You.*

### 1938
Elizabeth Bowen, *The Death of the Heart.*

John Dos Passos, *U.S.A.* Another odd work. Think about his structure. Why did he choose to present material this way?

Marjorie Kinnan Rawlings, *The Yearling.* This deceptively quiet book, as you know, was made into a successful film.

Muriel Rukeyser, *U.S. 1.*

Thornton Wilder, *Our Town.* This has been done to death. Why? Because it is so accessible.

### 1939
Moss Hart and George S. Kaufman, *The Man Who Came to Dinner.*

Lillian Hellman, *The Little Foxes.* By now, the South was center stage in American literature.

Katherine Anne Porter, *Pale Horse, Pale Rider.*

William Saroyan, *The Time of Your Life.* Can you make the connection between *U.S.A., Our Town,* and this work?

John Steinbeck, *The Grapes of Wrath.*

Dalton Trumbo, *Johnny Got His Gun.*

Nathanael West, *The Day of the Locust.*

### 1940
Arthur Koestler, *Darkness at Noon.*

Carson McCullers, *The Heart Is a Lonely Hunter.* People back in Columbus, Georgia, wouldn't speak to Carson after reading her books.

Christina Stead, *The Man Who Loved Children.*

James Thurber and Elliott Nugent, *The Male Animal.*

### 1941
Noel Coward, *Blithe Spirit.*

Eudora Welty, *A Curtain of Green and Other Stories.* People in Jackson, Mississippi, did and still do speak to Ms. Welty. On the surface she is gentle, but her themes are not slight. Her voice, while very Southern, is quite different from the other celebrated Southern authors of this time.

### 1942
Sir Rabindranath Tagore (d. 1941), *Poems*, edited by Krishna Kripalani.

Thornton Wilder, *The Skin of Our Teeth.*

### 1943
Edna St. Vincent Millay, *Collected Lyrics.*

Delmore Schwartz, *Genesis: Book One.* Most definitely not a Southern voice.

### 1944
S. J. Perelman and Ogden Nash (music by Kurt Weill), *One Touch of Venus.*

Sir Osbert Sitwell, *Left Hand! Right Hand!* The Sitwell siblings strike again.

### 1945
Walter de la Mare, *The Burning Glass and Other Poems.*

Nancy Mitford, *The Pursuit of Love.* I still don't think the English have recovered from the Mitford sisters.

George Orwell (pseudonym for Eric Arthur Blair), *Animal Farm: A Fairy Story.*

Tennessee Williams, *The Glass Menagerie.*

Richard Wright, *Black Boy.*

## 1946

Christopher Isherwood, *The Berlin Stories.*

Carson McCullers, *The Member of the Wedding.*

Terence Rattigan, *The Winslow Boy.*

Robert Penn Warren, *All the King's Men.*

Frank Yerby, *The Foxes of Harrow.* He was a popular novelist.

## 1947

Malcolm Lowry, *Under the Volcano.*

Sean O'Faolain, *Teresa.*

S. J. Perelman, *The Best of Perelman.*

Tennessee Williams, *A Streetcar Named Desire.*

## 1948

Hortense Calisher, *In the Absence of Angels.*

Truman Capote, *Other Voices, Other Rooms.* Like a comet, this beautiful talent reduced himself to dust.

Ezra Pound, *Cantos.* There is nothing easy about Ezra Pound, but you can't afford to ignore his work.

James Thurber, *The Beast in Me and Other Animals.*

Gore Vidal, *The City and the Pillar.* This was a concern, a style, left behind by Vidal.

## 1949

Truman Capote, *A Tree of Night and Other Stories.*

Christopher Fry, *The Lady's Not for Burning.*

## 1950

William Inge, *Come Back Little Sheba.*

Carl Sandburg, *Complete Poems.* He styled himself a poet of the people.

Isaac Bashevis Singer, *The Family Moskat.*

Tennessee Williams, *The Roman Spring of Mrs. Stone.*

William Butler Yeats (d. 1939), *Collected Poems.*

## 1951

Langston Hughes, *Mortgage of a Dream Deferred.*

J. D. Salinger, *The Catcher in the Rye.* Will this stand the test of time? We won't know.

## 1952

Ralph Ellison, *The Invisible Man.*

Ernest Hemingway, *The Old Man and the Sea.*

Mary McCarthy, *The Groves of Academe.* She doesn't write with a pen. She uses a scalpel! Here is a writer with terrific control—what does that do to the material?

## 1953

James Baldwin, *Go Tell It on the Mountain.*

Arthur Miller, *The Crucible.*

Ogden Nash, *The Private Dining Room and Other New Verses.*

Mary Renault (pseudonym for Mary Challans), *The Charioteer.* She has a huge cult following. Think about the material. In another writer's hands this novel would have died. As it is, the tone of the book is a problem, at least, for me.

## 1954

William Golding, *Lord of the Flies.*

Dylan Thomas, *Under Milk Wood: A Play for Voices*. You've probably read this.

1955

Vladimir Nabokov, *Lolita*. Another non-native writer who wrote in English. He is important to study for his use of our language and for his themes. Would an American have selected this? What about an English writer? If they had, imagine how they would have presented the story. Why was/is he so celebrated? Does Cold War politics have anything to do with it?

Sir Terence Rattigan, *Separate Tables* (two plays).

Tennessee Williams, *Cat on a Hot Tin Roof*.

1956

James Baldwin, *Giovanni's Room*.

Brendan Behan, *The Quare Fellow*.

Allen Ginsberg, *Howl and Other Poems*.

Eugene O'Neill, *Long Day's Journey into Night*.

1957

Stanley Kunitz, *Selected Poems, 1928–1958*.

John Osborne, *Look Back in Anger*.

1958

Archibald MacLeish, *J.B.: A Play in Verse*. Much admired at that time.

C. P. Snow, *The Conscience of the Rich*.

Tennessee Williams, *Garden District: Something Unspoken* and *Suddenly Last Summer*.

1959

John Ciardi, *39 Poems*.

Lorraine Hansberry, *A Raisin in the Sun*.

Grace Paley, *The Little Disturbances of Man.*

Muriel Spark, *Memento Mori.* Quite a wicked little book, displaying Spark's distinctive characteristics as a writer.

### 1960

Harper Lee, *To Kill a Mockingbird.*

Brian Moore, *The Luck of Ginger Coffey.*

Tillie Olsen, *Tell Me a Riddle.*

Harold Pinter, *The Birthday Party and Other Plays.*

Sylvia Plath, *The Colossus and Other Poems.*

Anne Sexton, *To Bedlam and Part Way Back.*

Gary Snyder, *Myths and Texts.*

### 1961

Muriel Spark, *The Prime of Miss Jean Brodie.* You probably know this one.

### 1962

Edward Albee, *Who's Afraid of Virginia Woolf?* Caused a sensation when first produced. Would it today?

Doris Lessing, *The Golden Notebook.* She has passionate admirers. Your reaction to her work ought to tell you something about the kind of books you want to write.

### 1963

Hortense Calisher, *Extreme Magic: A Novella and Other Stories.*

### 1964

James Dickey, *Two Poems of the Air.*

Denise Levertov, *O Taste and See: New Poems.*

Robert Lowell, *For the Union Dead.* This harks back to another Lowell.

## 1965
May Sarton, *Mrs. Stevens Hears the Mermaids Singing.*

## 1966
Truman Capote, *In Cold Blood: A True Account of a Multiple Murder and Its Consequences.* A twist: nonfiction treated almost like fiction. You're on dangerous ground here. After Capote this "form" took off. The form makes me uneasy. I feel that it is intrinsically dishonest.

Barnard Malamud, *The Fixer.*

## 1967
Marianne Moore, *The Complete Poems.*

Joyce Carol Oates, *A Garden of Earthly Delights.*

Joe Orton, *Crimes of Passion: The Ruffian on the Stair, and The Erpingham Camp.* Why did this kind of drama come forth in England? Something happened there after World War II.

Tom Stoppard, *Rosencrantz and Guildenstern Are Dead.* Gilbert used Rosencrantz and Guildenstern in 1892. What's the pull of these two Shakespearean characters?

William Styron, *The Confessions of Nat Turner.*

Thornton Wilder, *The Eighth Day.* This is an interesting "failure."

## 1968
Gore Vidal, *Myra Breckinridge.*

## 1969
John Berryman, *Dream Songs.*

Kurt Vonnegut, *Slaughterhouse Five, or, The Children's Crusade.*

## 1970
Maya Angelou, *I Know Why the Caged Bird Sings.* Maya is still singing, thank God.

Enid Bagnold, *Four Plays.*

Denise Levertov, *Relearning the Alphabet.*

## 1971
Cynthia Ozick, *The Pagan Rabbi and Other Stories.*

## 1972
Barbara Deming, *Wash Us and Comb Us.* This is a personal book, essays disguised as memoirs. Pay attention to her style.

James Merrill, *Braving the Elements.* A style 180 degrees from Deming—yet, how are these writers similar?

## 1973
Adrienne Rich, *Diving into the Wreck: Poems 1971–1972.*

Gore Vidal, *Burr.* Gore Vidal uses history as a mirror for the political life in the 1970's. Even if you don't "get" it, the book reads well as a story about Burr. This has Vidal's trademark: superb structure, suspicion/fear of emotion. Also, this is a good example of a book in which something is withheld from you until the end without its being a trick. It relates to the emotional blindness/innocence of the main character.

## 1975
Seamus Heaney, *Bog Poems.*

Ruth Prawer Jhabvala, *Heat and Dust.*

## 1976
W. H. Auden, *Collected Poems.*

## 1980
Margaret Drabble, *The Middle Ground.*

## 1981
Anthony Burgess, *Earthly Powers.*

Please excuse the lacunae from 1981 until today. I am weary. I've read many recently published novels, but with the exception of

*The Color Purple* by Alice Walker, I'm drawing a blank. Of course, right now there is an avalanche of books being published and I know I've missed some fine ones. The closer one gets to one's own time the harder it is to see clearly.

For a copy of the complete reading list, send a check (no cash, please) for ten dollars made out to Speakeasy, Inc., to:

Speakeasy, Inc.
P.O. Box 4671
Charlottesville, VA 22905

This covers the cost of printing, paper, and first-class mailing.

RITA MAE BROWN was born in Hanover, Pennsylvania, and grew up in Florida. She earned a degree in Classics and English from New York University and a doctorate in Political Science from the Institute for Policy Studies in Washington, D.C.

She has published several books of poems, a translation of six medieval Latin plays, seven novels—*Rubyfruit Jungle, In Her Day, Six of One, Southern Discomfort, Sudden Death, High Hearts,* and *Bingo*—and a writers' manual, *Starting from Scratch.* She has been twice nominated for an Emmy, for her scripts *I Love Liberty* and *The Long Hot Summer.*

She lives in Charlottesville, Virginia.